英语口语阶梯晋级系列

全新版

中级

大胆开口说英语

主 编：刘 力

主 审：Joe Wisham［美］

副主编：吕 爽 胡 洁

编 者：付晶晶 吴 萍

Dare to Open Your Mouth

第2版

西安交通大学出版社

XI'AN JIAOTONG UNIVERSITY PRESS

U0121825

内 容 提 要

《全新版大胆开口说英语》（第2版）中级，共涵盖十个单元，内容涉及：提建议，描述人物，事件或经历，新闻评论等。每个单元分别包含五个板块：① Learning objectives（单元目标）：介绍本单元的学习目标，帮助教师和学生检验其学习成果。② Getting started（跃跃欲试）：通过2～3个练习，导入本单元相关技能的学习。③ Let's talk（说说看）：通过提供音频、视频及阅读等材料，帮助学生学习和掌握相关技能。④ Comprehensive work（综合练习）：侧重训练学生的技能输出，加大口语练习的难度，集中反馈学习效果。⑤ Language focus（语言重点）：侧重归纳与单元主题相关的语言形式，为学生完成后续的口语任务提供语言准备。

本系列教材可供大学英语专业、非英语专业课堂教学和课外练习使用，也可作为非英语专业研究生的教学辅助学习材料；还可作为参加自学考试的学员、专科学生以及英语爱好者学习英语口语的书籍；亦可作为英语口语培训教材使用。

图书在版编目（CIP）数据

全新版大胆开口说英语：中级／刘力主编 .——2版

—— 西安：西安交通大学出版社，2018.8

（英语口语阶梯晋级系列）

ISBN 978-7-5693-0857-0

Ⅰ . ①全… Ⅱ . ①刘… Ⅲ . ①英语—口语—教材

Ⅳ . ① H319. 9

中国版本图书馆 CIP 数据核字（2018）第 207957 号

书　　名：	全新版大胆开口说英语 第2版（中级）
主　　编：	刘　力
图书策划：	王晓芬
责任编辑：	王晓芬

出版发行　西安交通大学出版社
　　　　　　（西安市兴庆南路 10 号邮政编码 710049）
网　　址：http://www.xjtupress.com
电　　话：(029) 82668357　82668851（发行中心）
　　　　　　(029) 82668315（总编办）
传　　真：(029) 82668857
印　　刷：陕西龙山海天艺术印务有限公司

开　　本：787mm×1092mm　1/16　印张9.25　字数 214 千字
版次印次：2018 年 10 月第 2 版　　2018 年 10 月第 1 次印刷
书　　号：ISBN 978-7-5693-0857-0
定　　价：32.00 元

读者购书、书店添货，如发现印装质量问题，请与本社发行中心联系、调换。
投稿热线：(029) 82668519　82668284　下载 PPT，请联系：475478288@qq.com
读者信箱：475478288@qq.com

前　言

2009 年第一版教材简介

　　《全新版大胆开口说英语》（初级、中级、高级）系列书第一版于 2009 年出版。该教材可为大学英语专业或非英语专业课堂使用，也可作为非英语专业研究生的教学辅助教材，或是参加自学考试的学生、专科学生以及英语爱好者学习英语口语的书籍。教材采用图文并茂的形式，从基本生存英语、情景交流会话、逐渐过渡到自由讨论和辩论。遵循贴近生活、生动具体、循序渐进的编写原则，对有效提高学习者的英语交际能力起着很大的促进作用。归纳起来，教材具有以下特点：

　　◆ 以输入促进输出。教材注重相关信息的输入，针对同一交际场景或话题，尽量多地提供多种应对方式所需的语言基本素材。

　　◆ 内容丰富、题材广泛。教材的话题覆盖面广，内容跨度大：既有与日常生活相关的话题，如衣食住行、社交礼节、风俗习惯、文娱体育等，也有与专门领域有关的话题，如经济贸易、教育环保、社会问题等。

　　◆ 实用性强，全方面培养学生的语言技能。教材内容贴近生活，文字材料或来自地道的英文报告，或由外籍教师根据场景精心设计，不仅为学习者提供了必要的语言输入，也便于学习者练习和模仿，使得学习者的口语表达不再停留在基本的语音语调等训练层面，而将会是言之有物，娓娓道来。

　　◆ 图文并茂、生动有趣。丛书中大量生动形象的图片资料，使得英语学习不再是枯燥无味。

2018 年第二版改版理念

　　随着时代的变化和发展，英语学习者的外语水平也普遍提高，由此对教学内容和教学方法也提出了更高的要求。为了适应外语教学的改革与发展、学生需求的巨变，我们对旧版教材在语言活动的目标、语言形式的新颖程度以及话题内容等方面进行全面修订，修订遵循以下思路：

继承旧版教材所秉承的实用性的理念。让学习者广泛接触题材、体裁、风格各异的语言输入，深度参与形式多样、难度由浅入深的学习任务，逐步以任务型语言教学为指导原则。任务型语言教学实际上是交际教学法理论在操作层面的落实，它不仅继承了交际教学法的语言观，还克服了其注重意义表达而忽视了语言形式的弱点。同时，经过几十年的时间，任务型教学已经形成了比较完整的操作体系，具有较高的外部效度，可以指导不同环境下的外语教学。

将能否激发学生的交际意愿作为教材内容选择的首要标准。在教材材料的选择方面主要有以下特点：第一，时代变化和社会发展对人们日常生活产生影响的；第二，可以从不同角度探讨，并且能引起年轻人思考的；第三，西方社会和文化现象中与中国社会和文化现象具有可比性的。这些话题的普适性强，容易引起学生的兴趣和思考，让他们有话想说，有话可说。全部材料均采用有实质内容的英文原文，口语技能讲解和练习紧密联系。

本系列教材特色：

除了保持旧版教材话题广泛、内容丰富、生动有趣的特点，新版教材还尝试增加以下特色：

◆学习任务目标清晰，为教学效果的评估提供客观依据。

◆确保不同的学习任务紧密联系，引导学生有效达到学习目标。

◆语言功能全面，任务真实适用。

◆多角度思维，多层次讨论，培养思辨创新能力。输入材料为学生展现多元视角，各层次的口语任务激发学生从多角度进行思考和讨论。

本系列教材构成：

本系列教材含三个分册，在提高学生日常口语交际能力的基础上，三个分册又各有侧重。初级分册侧重基础口语能力，全书以情景为中心，满足读者在生活中用英语交流的最基本需求。中级分册侧重提升学生的基本交际能力，学习者通过积极完成各类口语任务，频繁接触并使用同一交际功能，促进口语输出的完成。高级分册侧重培养学生的思辨创新能力和学术交流能力，为学习者提供丰富的输入材料，以及各类情境中的口语表达的架构和表达范本，培养学生对各类话题的识别、分析、总结和判断能力，从而能够做到"理论性思考，清晰地表达"。

《全新版大胆开口说英语》（第二版）中级共涵盖十个单元，涉及日常口语最需要的十个内容，具体包括：喜欢／不喜欢，提建议，怀疑和担忧，道歉，对比／比较，赞同和反对，邀请，描述人物、事件或经历，问题及解决方案，新闻评论等。每个单元分别包含以下五个板块：

◆ Learning objectives（单元目标）：该板块介绍本单元的学习目标，帮助教师和学生检验本单元的学习效果。

◆ Getting started（跃跃欲试）：该板块为认知导读，通过 2 到 3 个练习，导入本单元相关技能，激发学生已有的知识储备，并对将要学习的内容有所了解。

◆ Let's talk（说说看）：该板块以技能传授为核心目标，通过提供音频、视频及阅读等材料，帮助学生学习相关技能，并通过大量练习加强对这些技能的掌握。

◆ Comprehensive work（综合练习）：该板块侧重训练学生的技能输出，在前两个板块学习的基础上，加大口语练习的难度，综合各个技能，集中反馈学习效果。

◆ Language focus（语言重点）：该板块侧重归纳与单元主题相关的语言形式，主要涉及与话题相关的词汇和表达，为学生完成后续的口语任务提供语言准备。

教学建议

本教材共三册，每册可使用一个学期。由于教材每个部分紧密相关，因此教学过程中要确保每个部分的练习和口语任务都要完成。学生可在课前或课后阅读"单元目标"部分的具体任务，为本单元的口语学习做好准备，教师也可使用这部分评估学习效果。"跃跃欲试"板块旨在启发学生了解相关技能，一方面引导学生使用已掌握的知识，另一方面让学生了解本单元的新内容。"说说看"板块的重点是帮助学生完成学习目标，尤其强调不同语境中语言使用的恰当性。"综合练习"板块则是对前两个板块的糅合，从具体技能入手，让学生在较高难度的口语练习中，强化所学内容。同时，这个部分的练习需要学生进行独立思考，运用批判性思维分析问题、解决问题，旨在培养学生的基本学术素养。

本书在编写过程中，我们参阅了大量的权威性图书和文献，包括网上参考资料等（附参考文献），因各种原因，无法联系上参考资料的作者，编者在此对这些作者表示衷心的感谢！

2018 年 8 月

Table of Contents
目录

Unit 1　Likes and Dislikes

- Learn expressions of **likes** and **dislikes** 表达喜欢／不喜欢

- Learn to express **likes** and **dislikes** in different situations
不同的话题中表达喜欢／不喜欢

- Learn to give reasons when talking about **likes** and **dislikes**
给出喜欢／不喜欢的原因

喜欢？不喜欢？我该怎么说？

Section I Getting started

Activity 1

Look at the following pictures and talk to your partners which activity you like most and which one you like least. Give your reasons.

Activity 2

Listen to the dialogue and complete the blanks with the expressions of **likes** *and* **dislikes.**

J: Mary! What a surprise to see you here.

M: Small world! Long time no see.

J: Yeah, what have you been doing? I haven't heard anything about you since I saw you last year at the graduation party.

M: Really? But I have heard a lot about you. I heard you've found a good paying job, haven't you?

J: You're well informed.

M: I'm interested in knowing what you are thinking of that job.

J: To be honest, _____, _____ .

M: Can't you? _____. Don't you think money is an important factor which determines our choices of a job?

J: _____. But I hate earning money without using the knowledge I learned. It's just like committing crimes.

M: I'm sorry. I don't think I can give any advice.

J: Oh, Mary, what do you do?

M: I'm taking advanced study for a MA.

J: Terrific! How smart you are! _____?

M: _____. What I worry about is just the exam. But sometimes the college life is dull as usual.

J: I really envy（羡慕，嫉妒）you. I hope I could do half as well as you.

M: You're flattering（恭维，奉承）me! Well, I must be going.

J: Keep in touch.

Now check the expressions:

J	M
➤ It's boring. I can't stand it	➤ I'd prefer a job which can better my income
➤ Maybe lots of people are rather keen on money	➤ It's interesting and simple
➤ Do you have any fancy for that	

Activity 3

Work in pairs and take turns to act out the conversations.

Conversation 1

A: What are you going to do this weekend?

B: I'm going to go shopping and have a dinner in a music-themed restaurant.

A: Sounds great! I like shopping most!

B: Oh, would you like going with me?

A: Sure. And we can order our favorite desserts in the ice-cream shop afterwards.

Conversation 2

A: What would you like to do tonight?

B: Me? I am considering a movie. Do you ever go to the movies?

A: Of course, I am fond of going to the movies.

B: Well, let's go to the movies.

A: There's a good one: "Hidden".

B: Fine.

说说看！

Section Ⅱ Let's talk

Activity 1

*Listen to the conversation and fill in the box with the expressions of **likes** and **dislikes**.*

Jenny: Are you seeing the movie "Jane Eyre", adapted from the famous love novel?

John: No, I _____. They are not for me.

Jenny: Me neither. They are usually disappointing. But a lot of people _____. They think it is a good way to learn the classics.

John: Yea, only two kinds of people _____.

Jenny: Who are they?

John: Those who don't have to time to read books and those _____

_____.

Jenny: Exactly. I _____.

John: Me too. I think reading is much more entertaining.

Likes	Dislikes	Reasons

Activity 2

Interview at least 4 of your classmates about whether they like travelling or not. If they do, where do they like and why? If they don't, what are their reasons? Then prepare an oral presentation on the topic "Travelling". You can use the following Memory Bank if necessary.

Name	Like / Dislike	Reasons
Nancy	<ul><li>…I'm fond of travelling…</li><li>I like Qingdao most.</li></ul>	<ul><li>Interesting , challenging</li><li>Visit different places</li><li>Eexperience something different</li><li>It's a beautiful seaside city with marvelous buildings.</li></ul>

Activity 3

Work in groups of three. Student A chooses 1 item he / she likes most from the following list. Describe it and explain reasons why he / she likes it to other group members. Other students guess what the item is and take turns.

- a carpet

- a pair of red shoes

- an old CD

- a golden ring

- a calculator

- a digital watch

- a heart-shaped sticker

一起完成一项困难的任务吧！

Section III Comprehensive work

You are the director of the Board of Directors of Jazz Advertising, the most successful company in Los Angeles. Now the president of the company is 65 years old. He wants to retire and it is your responsibility to make sure that

the company is in good hands when he steps down. You are looking for a suitable successor to fill his shoes. Take a look at the candidates and decide which one you will choose as the successor. Tell the board who you like the most and who you like the least and try to persuade other members to agree with you. Then tell the class who you choose as the President and what your reasons are.

Betty Middle: Betty is the head of the marketing department. She is 55 years old, is married and has two children. She has worked with Jazz for 20 years. Mrs. Middle is diligent and often works 50 hours a week. She is old-fashioned, strict and critical of her colleagues. Betty is unpopular in the company because she is ambitious and selfish. She feels that change is bad.

Benny Hill: He is a 47-year-old sales manager. He has been divorced twice and has no children. He has worked with company for 10 years. Mr. Hill is an outgoing and generous man who is popular with his colleagues. He refuses to work on weekend because he feels rest is important so that he will work productively. Although satisfied with his present position, he will accept the job of president if offered. Mr. Hill has a lot of sales experience and he feels that the company should try to expand. He would like to invest more money and open offices in other cities.

JR Evans: Mr. Evans, 39 years old and single, is the manager of the financial department. He has been with Jazz for 8 years, and has been promoted four times. He is the youngest manager in the company, and is ambitious. His colleagues consider him untrustworthy, and his constant sucking to the boss makes him unpopular. Mr. Evans is efficient, and the financial department is running very well under his supervision. If promoted, he will cut back operations and reduce costs by laying off some employees. He doesn't believe in expansion. He feels the key to success is in reducing costs.

Blanche Sands: Mrs. Sands is the manager of the advertising department. She is 41 years old and is married with four children. She has been with the Jazz for 15 years and is a team player. Her creativity and talent as an advertiser have been very important in keeping the company ahead of the composition. Other companies made generous offers to attract her from Jazz. Blanche, however, believes that loyalty is important, and she refused all offers. She has no experience in finance or marketing, but is willing to learn. She would like to become President because she had many ideas on how to change and improve the company.

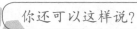

你还可以这样说？

Language Focus

Talking about **likes** 喜欢表达

- I like classical music a lot / very much.
- I came to like swimming.
- I've started to like Chinese food.
- I've come to like baseball.
- I love reading in my spare time.
- I enjoy walking alone in the park after dinner.
- I'm fond of reality shoe.
- I'm enthusiastic about play basketball.
- I can't find words to express how much I like it.

You can also use the following drills
表示喜欢的其他句型

- I'm keen on …
- I'm crazy about …
- I'm pleased with …
- I'm satisfied with …
- I'm interested in …
- I'm content with …
- I'm hooked on …
- I'm addicted to …
- I've developed a great liking for …
- I'm really a fan of …
- … grows on me.
- … appeals to me.
- … is my favorite.

Talking about **dislikes** 表达不喜欢

- I don't like eating alone.
- I don't particularly like speaking in public.
- I don't like the idea of travelling so long.
- I hate my boss!
- I dislike being yelled at.
- You don't seem like watching TV series.

You can also use the following drills

- I don't care for …
- I don't feel like …
- I'm nor fond of …
- I have a dislike of …
- I can't stand …
- I can hardly bear …
- I can't put up with …
- I can't say I like …
- I've got tired of …
- … is boring.
- … is just so-so.
- They make my stomach turn.
- They're not for me.
- I can't take it.
- It's driving me crazy.

Asking about **likes** and **dislikes** 询问别人是否喜欢

- Do you like roses?
- Do you like this writer in particular?
- Do you enjoy reading?
- Are you keen on stamp collection?
- Do you care for rock-and-roll?

You can also use the following drills.

- How about …?
- What about …?
- How do you like …?
- What do you think about / of …?
- What … do you like best?
- What is your favorite …?

Unit 2 Suggestions and Advice

 Objectives

- Learn expressions of giving suggestions 提出建议

- Learn to respond to suggestions 对别人的建议给出反馈

- Learn to give suggestions in different situations 给出喜欢／不喜欢的原因

怎么向别人提出建议？

Section I Getting started

 **Activity 1**

Look at the following pictures showing the situations Peter is in. Match the pictures to the responding suggestions. Try to give more suggestions to Peter.

- It is advised to make a balance between entertaining and study.
- It is moral to return the lost item to the owner.
- Respecting the old generation is a tradition in China.
- Saving money is a kind of self-discipline.

Activity 2

Listen to the dialogue and complete the blanks with the expressions of suggestions.

A: Hi, Mary. You look worried. What happened?

B: Well, I'm thinking of changing my job. _____ ?

A: My boss hates me, you know. And I couldn't take working the graveyard shift anymore.

B: Oh, man, _____ .
It's hard to find a job now. And you are well paid.

A: I see. But, _____ , anyway, it can't be solved. Now, _____ .

B: Mm, _____ ? Many people do that nowadays.

A: _____ . I will try that. Another drink?

B: No thanks. I have to go. So long.

A: So long.

Options:

1. I need you advice on the job	6. Don't rush to a decision
2. Sounds good	7. You are fond of your job now
3. Would you like to give me some advice	8. I would suggest you talk with your boss to solve the problem
4. That's impossible	9. You're tired of your job
5. Hard to explain	10. what about surfing on the Net to find job vacancies

 Activity 3

Listen to the conversations and underline the expressions of suggestions. Act them out in turns.

Conversation 1

A: I'm confused about what major I should choose.

B: What are you interested in?

A: Let me see. I'm interested in marketing and E-commerce. Oh, I also like English very much.

B: Mm, I would suggest that you major in marketing. Marketing is so important these days and all companies take marketing as one of their most important departments.

A: I agree, but I'd also like to take up a foreign language.

B: English? Sure, you can take English as your minor (副修科目). You know, English will be a vital skill in your future job-hunting in globalization.

A: Good! Thank you very much. Your suggestions are very helpful for me.

Conversation 2

A: Chew, the weekend is here at last. I really need to relax. What shall we do today?

B: I don't really know. Do you have any ideas?

A: Well, I need a new skirt. How about going shopping and hunting around with me if you have free time on your hands?

B: Oh, no! I just went shopping yesterday with Flora.

A: What a pity! What can we do then?

B: Why don't we have a big dinner in the new restaurant? I heard the food in the new restaurant tastes very delicious.

A: Marvelous! I am also considering treating myself. Shall we meet at the front gate at about 6 o'clock?

B: Good! See you.

试试提出建议吧！请给出你的原因。

Section II Let's talk

 **Activity 1**

Imagine you are preparing a surprising party for your friend. You are discussing with your other friends about: what present to buy, what things to prepare for the party and what activities to play at the party. You can use the following format.

A: What presents should we buy for Kathy's birthday?

B: Let's buy a notebook.

A: But she's just got a new one. How about …?

A: What do we buy for the party?

B: Let's buy some hamburgers!

A: Good. And what about …?

A: OK, then, let's see what activities to play.

B: Why don't we play cards?

C: Great! That must be funny.

D: …

Activity 2

Talk with your partners. Make some suggestions about reading a book and take turns.

A: Hello, Kelly! What are you going to do?

B: I'm going to the library to borrow a novel.

A: Great! What novel are you going to borrow?

B: Frankly, I have no idea. I just want to read a kind of love story. Do you have any suggestion?

A: How about _____?

B: Sounds interesting. What's the book about?

A: It's mainly tells _____.

B: Oh, so sad! I don't like such sad story. Can you recommend a story with a happy ending?

A: Well, _____.

B: No, but I've heard it many times.

A: _____.

B: All right. I will borrow this book right now. Thanks a lot !

A: _____.

Activity 3

Make up a dialogue with your partners in the following settings.

1. Asking for advice of your future major in university.

2. Asking for advice of life in college.

3. Giving suggestions of travelling in your hometown.

4. Giving suggestions of choosing association in college.

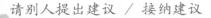

请别人提出建议 ／ 接纳建议

Section III Comprehensive work

Activity 1

Work in groups of three. You are planning a camping trip. Discuss with your partners about the possible situations you may be in and take turns to make suggestions to other group members.

Possible situations:

◆ the trip will be about 4 days in the filed

◆ hot during the daytime, about 35°C at noon

◆ much cooler at night and occasional rain

◆ someone may get hurt and there is no doctor

◆ no ready-meals

Activity 2

There is a meeting of the University Appointments Committee. On the agenda is the award of this year's Finance Scholarship. Four students have attained similar marks in the entrance exam. They have all applied for the scholarship.

Candidate 1:

John Smith Aged 17, not of outstanding natural ability but very hard-working. He made a good impression, but a little nervous at the whole idea of Finance school and the effects of the school may

have on his future career.

Candidate 2:

Kathy Green Aged 19, brilliant but not very hard-working. A likeable personality. Very musical, has funded and runs a pop-group.

Candidate 3:

Carol Anderson Aged 18, a quiet, attractive girl, responsible and able, but rather pliable in character. She has one older brother and three little sisters. She has to take them when necessary.

Candidate 4:

Edward Braun Aged 19, the son and grandson of financiers. Enthusiastic, ambitious and career-minded. Parents won't finance his studies. In character rather aggressive and quick-tempered, but generous, a good friend.

你还可以这样说！

Language Focus

Asking for suggestions

- Do you have any suggestions?
- Can you recommend a pen?
- What do you think seeing a movie tonight?
- I need your advice on choosing optional courses.
- I was wondering if you could recommend a good teacher.
- You've got any good idea?
- I don't know what to do. I need your suggestions.
- I wish you could give me your suggestions.

Offering suggestions

- Can I offer a suggestion?
- Why don't you trying this jacket?
- How about having dinner with them?
- What about this shirt?
- How does Japanese food sound?
- Don't you think we should take this toy?
- I think you'd better going there in person.
- It might be a good idea to visit the church.
- If I were you, I would go there by train.
- Maybe you should call the hotel to book a room.

Responding to Suggestions

- Sounds great!
- Cool!
- Good idea!
- Excellent suggestion. I will try it.
- I'll keep that in my mind.
- Maybe you are right.
- I hadn't thought of that.
- That couldn't occur to me.
- It's easier said than done.
- I am not sure of it, but thanks all the same.
- I don't think there is any possibility.
- I'm afraid it is not acceptable.

Unit 3　Doubts and Worries

Objectives

● Learn expressions of signifying doubts and worries 表达怀疑和担忧

● Learn to explain reasons for doubts 解释为何担忧

● Learn to encourage and reassure someone in bad mood or in trouble 安抚鼓励，消除疑虑

负面情绪的地道表达

Section 1　Getting started

Activity 1

Read the idioms and expressions below and match them with the mood they're describing.

1. She got *bent out of shape* over the new dress code at work.	frustration
2. After the accident she was completely *shaken up*.	worry
3. We were *on pins and needles* waiting to hear if we won the contest.	depression
4. Sorry, I can't do the chores today, I'm *beat / bushed*!	fear

5. It *drives me up the wall* when people answer their cell phones in English class.	despair
6. I've had a terrible day at work and I'm feeling completely *fed up*!	anxiety
7. The look in the prisoner's eye made my *blood run cold*!	being exhausted
8. He's *at his wits' end*. He's tried everything to solve the problem, nothing has worked.	boredom
9. When she left him, he was *down in the dumps* for a couple of weeks.	anger
10. When her son went missing, she was *beside herself with worry*.	shock

Activity 2

Read the quotes below and discuss with your partner about something that you don't believe in and explain the reasons for your doubt.

➤ " *I don't believe in failure. It is not failure if you enjoyed the process.*"

— Oprah Winfrey

➤ " *I don't believe in luck… it's persistence, hard work, and not forgetting your dream.*"

— Janet Jackson

➤ " *By simple common sense, I don't believe in God, in none.*"

— Charlie Chaplin

➤ " *I don't believe there is any true friendship without a bond of honor, and the honor in friendship is the respect you give the other that she also gives you.*"

— Dorothy Allison

➤ " I don't believe in taking right decisions. I take decisions and make them right."

— Ratan Tata

➤ " I don't believe in the kind of magic in my books. But I do believe that something very magical can happen when you read a good book."

— J.K. Rowling

➤ " I don't believe in intuition. When you get sudden flashes of perception, it's just the brain working faster than usual. But you've been getting ready to know it for a long time, and when it comes, you feel you've known it always."

— Katherine Anne Porter

Activity 3

Choose the answer to each question below to test your level of anxiety and exchange the result with your partner. Try to provide a way to relieve his / her anxiety.

Q1: How do people think of you?	A. Most people have the same views as I do. B. Different people see me differently. C. I'm not sure and also don't care.
Q2: What do you think other people's opinion about you?	A. Similar to mine. B. Will influence my own opinion. C. Has nothing to do with me.

Q3: What do you often feel about your true self?	A. I'll try to be myself under any circumstance. B. I can be what I am more freely without acquaintances around. C. I have to know myself from other people's eyes.
Q4: What do you always have in mind?	A. My life is regular and normal with little anxiety. B. Anxiety is not a bad thing and keeps me going on. C. I'm always anxious because I didn't reach my goal.
Q5: Are you clear about the purpose of doing anything in most cases?	A. Very clear B. Not so clear C. Very unclear
Q6: How do you feel most of the time when you're together with friends?	A. Relaxed. B. Nervous, because I haven't still finished my work. C. I don't want to stay there any longer.
Q7: What do you think of your life?	A. I'm satisfied because I've got what I want. B. Sometimes I'll doubt the meaning of life. C. I'm nothing but a studying / working machine.
Q8: How do you feel about your study / work?	A. What I'm doing is worthwhile. B. It's just for earning a living. C. Suspicious of its meaning.

Q9: How do you feel like dating with a person?	A. Know exactly what my favorite type is. B. Are prone to turn my nose up at him / her owing to some details. C. Feel irritable because I cannot find a suitable mate.

对意外之事难以置信；对焦虑之人安抚鼓励。

Section II Let's talk

Activity 1

Read the following situation and choose appropriate sentences to complete the dialogue.

(Setting: Gordon visits Emma's house. They talk about one piece of striking news about their schoolmate Terry Brown.）

E: Good evening, Gordon.

G: Good evening, Emma. What are you doing now?

E: I'm surfing the net.

G: Have you got anything interesting?

E: Yes. _____Terry Brown has achieved the Award of Excellence by the Microsoft this month?

G: Oh my goodness! You've got to be kidding. _____ !
    I simply can't believe what you've said.

27

E: _____?

G: As a matter of fact, he is not an excellent student in our school. He never studies very hard.

E: In the beginning, I also rather doubted him. But _____, we must admit.

G: _____. Maybe we don't know him very much.

E: Yes. We shouldn't judge a person just by his appearance.

G: Sounds reasonable. _____

_____.

Options:

1. I am still thinking whether this is true	6. We must believe that every person is able to make progress
2. It is beyond doubt	7. Are you sure that
3. What's wrong with you	8. It's incredible
4. Why don't you believe what I have said	9. I'm feeling pretty confident about it
5. That's easier said than done	10. Do you believe that

Activity 2

Make a simulation dialogue with your partner based on the following scenarios.

1. Bob who has never passed exams in primary school became a college professor.

2. Michael who was slow and felt inferior is running for Mayor and very likely to win.

3. Greg who is weak and handicapped won the championship of the marathon.

Activity 3

Listen to a conversation between a man and a woman. Discuss with your partner on how to express your comfort, encouragement and sympathy to someone who is anxious and worried by grouping the responses with letter C (comfort), E (encouragement) and S (sympathy) . Then role play a conversation based on the following situation: you are worrying about an interview for a part-time job this weekend. You're so anxious that you even stammer. Your partner is trying to comfort you and give you some encouragement.

1. A: I'm afraid I'll definitely fail this time.

    B: Oh, poor thing!   ☐
        Better luck next time!   ☐
        Don't give it another thought. ☐

2. A: The new project makes me uneasy.

    B: Everything will be fine.   ☐
        I feel sorry for you.   ☐
        You can do it.   ☐

3. A: How could this horrible thing happen to me!

    B: It must be tough for you.   ☐
        Things will work out.   ☐
        I'll cross my fingers.   ☐

4. A: I'm really awful at the interview.

    B: Look on the bright side.   ☐
        I understand the way you feel.   ☐
        Don't take it too seriously!   ☐

5. A: I'm pretty worried about the result of the employee evaluation.

    B: You have my sympathy.   ☐
        Nothing to worry about.   ☐
        Hey, cheer up!   ☐

在讨论中分享态度，排忧解难。

Section III Comprehensive work

Activity 1

Look at the picture and discuss in a group the questions below.

Questions:

• Do you always believe those
  beggars in the street?

• What's your attitude towards
  them?

Activity 2

Watch a video clip about a boy named Charlie Brown who has several run-ins with the kite. Then work in groups discussing the following questions: How can you tackle the things that annoy you over and over again? What would you say to reassure your friend if he or she worries too much?

https://www.youtube.com/watch?v=SzNoOyI0NoA

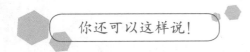

你还可以这样说!

Language Focus

Expressing Doubts 表达疑虑

- I doubt that / whether …
- I wonder that / whether …
- I don't believe / trust …
- I think … is hard to believe.
- I have little confidence in …
- I am not certain (sure) …
- I am in doubt (about) …
- I am still thinking whether this is true.

- I can hardly believe / imagine it.
- I know better than that!
- I won't buy it / that story.
- I wouldn't bet on it.
- I smell a rat.
- I don't take … too seriously.
- You've got to be kidding.
- You must be joking.
- You are not serious, aren't you?
- It's fool's trick to trust your words.
- It's unlikely that …
- It couldn't be … but …
- It's doubtful / incredible / chancy / iffy!
- It sounds fishy / suspicious / funny to me.
- It's too good to be true.
- It's so unbelievably good that there has to be something wrong.
- It can't be!
- Nothing this good happens, it must be a mistake.
- Goodness me! It's unbelievable.
- That's hard to believe.
- That's easier said than done.
- How is that possible?
- Do you really believe …?
- Do you believe in …?
- Do you mean it?
- Are you serious?
- Are you joking / kidding?
- Don't pull my leg.

- Tell me another.
- Get on with you!
- Give me a break!

Expressing Beliefs 表达相信／信服

- I believe / trust / accept / suppose …
- I feel confident of …
- I have great beliefs in …
- I have complete faith in …
- I have no doubt of …
- I think … is true / believable / credible / convincible.
- I take your word.
- I am convinced / sure of ….
- I am sure / certain that …
- I'm feeling pretty confident about it.
- I bet …
- I give full credit to …
- It is beyond doubt.
- You can rely on …
- That's where I am.

Expressing Worries 表达担忧

- Anything wrong?
- Are you OK / all right / ant better / feeling better?
- Is anything bothering you?
- Do you have anything on your mind?
- What's wrong with you?
- What's up / wrong / the matter / the problem (with you)?
- What are you worried about?
- What's going on?
- What's worrying you?
- Why are you so glum（闷闷不乐）?
- You look serious / grave.
- You look so down / sad / gloomy（令人沮丧的，悲欢的）/ glum.
- You don't look very happy.
- You look exhausted / very tired / worn-out / bushed（疲倦的）/ pooped（筋疲力竭的）.
- You're not yourself today.
- You seem different today.
- You've got the blues.
- I'm (pretty / rather / deeply / a little) worried / concerned / anxious about …

- I'm afraid …
- I'm really awful at …
- I'm on pins and needles（发麻，针刺感）.
- I can't help worrying.
- I can't get rid of my worries.

- I know I'm being silly, but I'll worry about … for the rest of my life.
- It has always been a worry to me.
- It is very worrisome.
- It makes me uneasy.
- It is a real worry to …
- How could it happen to me!
- What should I do!

Expressing Reassurance 表达安慰鼓励；消除疑虑

- What a pity / shame!
- How awful / sad!
- What bad luck!
- Don't worry / be concerned (about it).
- Don't blame yourself.
- Don't take it too seriously.
- Don't get worked up over nothing!
- Don't feel so bad about yourself.
- Don't be so hard / down on yourself.

- Don't be a chicken / coward / sissy.
- Don't give it another thought.
- No need to get so worked up.
- Nothing to worry about.

- Never mind! / No big deal! / Forget about it! / Take it easy!
- Let's face it / Let's be realistic.
- It' nothing that you should worry about.
- It wasn't your fault.
- It happens / it's a common mistake!
- It's okay / no problem / all right / nothing.
- Things will work out. / Things will turn out fine.
- Everything will be OK / fine.
- Your condition is not as bad as that.
- I've seen worse.
- It could / might have been worse.

- Cheer up / Come on / Pull yourself together / Get it together!
- Get a hold of yourself / Get your shit together!
- Keep your chin up / Keep it up!
- Go for it / Take a chance!
- Hang in there / Don't give it up / Keep at it!
- Look on the bright side.
- Try harder next time.
- Have another try / Give it another try / Try and do it.
- You can do anything if you really want to / put your mind to it.
- You can accomplish anything if you believe in it / are so minded.
- There's a chance / possibility.
- It could happen.
- I wish you success / Success to you / May you succeed!
- I'll have my finger crossed / I'll cross my fingers.
- I'll keep my hopes up.

- I'm sorry about that / to hear that.
- I feel really bad about it.
- I (quite) understand the way you feel.
- I know how you feel / I feel for you.
- I know how you are hurting.
- I really sympathize with you / You have my sympathy.
- That's too bad / a pity / unfortunate.
- Tough luck.
- Oh, poor thing!
- It must be tough for you / It must be hard on you.

Unit 4 Apologies

 Objectives

- Learn expressions of apologizing on different topics
  就不同话题向他人道歉

- Learn to explain your misbehavior and give your promise
  解释为何担忧

- Learn to respond to apologies
  回应他人的道歉

不同场合中如何向他人道歉。

Section I Getting started

 **Activity 1**

Suppose you are in the following situations. Make apologies or respond to others' apologies. You can follow the model if necessary.

Situation 1

You're having dinner in a restaurant and you accidently spilled a cup coffee to the friend who sits beside you. Make an apology to your friend and offer to clean the clothes for him / her.

Situation 2

You made an appointment to your teacher one week before. But you forgot this appointment and didn't make it. Call your teacher to make an apology and make another appointment.

Situation 3

You and your friends are watching a football match together at your home at late night. Your neighbor knocks the door and complains that you make too much noise to disturb them. Make an apology and make a promise that you will never do that again.

Model:

A: *Sorry to bother you, sir. But I have something urgent to do. Would you like to hurry, please?*

B: *Okay. I'll be finished right now.*

A: *Thanks. Sorry about the inconvenience.*

B: *Never mind.*

Activity 2

Listen to the dialogue and complete the blanks with the expressions of apologies.

Brian didn't attend the company meeting yesterday. This morning, he went to the manager and apologized for that.

B: Good morning, Ms. Lee.

L: Good morning, Brian. Why all this hurry?

B: _____.

L: _____? You've done a good job.

B: Thanks for saying that. But please _____

_____.

I caught a bad could and had to see the doctor.

L: _____. It can happen to anyone. Well, we had to hold the meeting without you, though.

B: I appreciate your kindness.

L: _____! Anything I can be of help?

B: Yes, could you tell me how you would consider my proposal about the reform of our Sales Department?

L: Proposal? _____. I will take it into proper consideration soon.

B: Well, that's all right. _____.

L: _____. See you later.

B: See you!

Options:

1. Forgive me for not attending company meeting yesterday afternoon	6. Excuse me for not discussing that at the meeting
2. I'd like to apologize to you	7. Forget it
3. I'm sorry to have disturbed you	8. What for
4. I have something to tell you	9. That's OK
5. I had a high fever and the doctor told me to stay in bed	10. There is really no need to apologize for that

Activity 3

Read the conversations and underline the expressions of apologies.

1. A: Hello, Bob. How was your weekend?

   B: Great! What about you? Did you go back home?

   A: No. I didn't. My term paper is due today. So I had to spend two days finishing it. But I made it. By the way, did you get me that sports magazine from the bookstore downtown?

   B: Oh, gosh! What a poor memory I have! I forgot all about it. I'm terribly sorry, Steve.

   A: It doesn't matter. I can borrow it form George. He buys every issue.

2. A: Hi, Nancy. Please wait. I've got something to tell you.

   B: Yea, what is it, Stella?

   A: Well, I was invited to a dance last night. As it was my first invitation to a college party, I really wanted to impress people there. I needed a beautiful dress so badly, but my clothes are all way too casual. I meant to borrow one from you, but you went home for the weekend. So I took the liberty and wore that black backless dress of yours to the party. I know I shouldn't have done so. I hope you'll accept my apologies, Nancy.

   B: Oh, that's OK, Stella. At least you had a good tome!

   A: Yea, I did. Thank you, Nancy. That's so kind of you!

3. A: Good afternoon. Professor Thompson.

   B: Good afternoon, William.

   A: Oh, Professor Thompson …

B: Yes?

A: I have to apologize for my carelessness. I was doing an experiment in the lab this afternoon when I heard the telephone ring. As I hurried to answer it, my elbow bumped one of the test tubes you placed on the shelf. It felt off and smashed. I feel bad because I was so careless.

B: Oh, no, don't blame yourself! I should have put them in the test-tube stand. It's not your fault.

向别人道歉并解释你的不当行为。

Section II Let's talk

Activity 1

Imagine you are apologizing for making noise to your neighbor. You can use the following expressions in your conversation.

➢ I've come to apologize.

➢ I'm sorry. I didn't realize it was that loud.

➢ I promise I'll keep it down in the future.

Activity 2

You are the new assistant of your boss John and not familiar with your job. Your boss is angry with what you have done and you are making *apologies to John. Make up a conversation with your partner. You can use the expressions below.*

John

- Look at the letter! What a mass it is!

- Didn't you read the letter before you sent it to me?

- Can't you find these mistakes?

- How can you litter in the room!

- It's the basic rule that the office should be clean and neat!

- The paper! The pens! The mails! Everywhere!

- If you can't improve your job, I have to fire you.

- I mean it!

You

- I'm awfully sorry.

- You cannot believe how sorry I am.

- I'm sorry for what I have done.

- I honestly didn't mean it that way.

- It was stupid of me. I really do apologize.

- I will never do that again!

- I promise I will make it up to you.

Activity 3

Make up a dialogue with your partners in the following settings.

1. On a crowded bus, you stepped on a passenger's toe.

2. You had to miss a get-together with your best friend.

3. You broke a vase when you are in your friend's home.

4. You lost the book you borrowed from your classmate.

向别人道歉／回应别人的道歉

Section III Comprehensive work

Activity 1

Work in groups of three to give a performance. It's a play consisting of two scenes. There are three characters: a customer, a clerk, and a sales manager. The story happens in a shopping mall.

Scene 1: the customer and the clerk

● The customer bought a computer for his son.

● The customer complained angrily when he turned on the computer, large dots would be flashed at the edges of the screen.

● The clerk apologized.

● The customer demands a refund.

- The clerk asked him to show the receipt but the man lost it.

- They quarreled.

Scene 2: the customer and the sales manager

- The manager apologized for the manner of the clerk.

- The manager offered solution to the problem.

- The customer agreed to repair the computer.

- It would take 3 weeks to repair it and the customer got anger.

- The manager apologized again and offered rent a computer free of charge.

 Activity 2

Work in pairs. *You will receive a card, describing a situation you are in. You are allowed 15 minutes for discussion of the situation and for a first run-through of the improvisation. Each member of a pair should play both roles.*

> You invited your best friend to your birthday party last month. He has not invited you to his party next week. You have bought him a nice present. You meet him in the street and he does not mention his birthday.

You and your sister share a car. She wants to use it tonight to take her latest boyfriend to a party. You need it to get to a late business meeting in the next town.

An old lady is having a long personal conversation with the clerk at the village post office. There is a queue of busy people waiting behind her, include you.

You work on the night shift and need to sleep during the day. Every afternoon for the last week, the neighbors' children have played football against the wall of your house. They have just woken you up again.

brought drinks

near you but not to

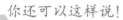
你还可以这样说!

Language Focus

Making an apology

- I'm so awfully / terribly sorry.
- Please forgive me.
- I hope you can excuse me.
- Please accept my sincere apology.
- I can't tell you how sorry I am.
- Words can't describe how sorry I am.
- I just don't know what to say.
- I really feel bad about it.

pology.

am.

ow sorry I am.

t to say.

ad about it.

Apologizing for mistakes

- I'm sorry for what I've done.
- I shouldn't have done that.
- I should have asked you first.
- I honestly didn't mean it.
- I didn't mean to do it.
- I didn't mean it that way.
- I don't know how that could have happened.
- You were right and I was wrong.
- It's all my fault. I'll try to make it up to you.
- My mistake. It won't happen again.
- It was so stupid of me. I really do apologize.
- I owe you an apology for what I did yesterday.

Accepting apologies

- That's all right.
- You're forgiven.
- That's OK.
- No harm done.
- Never mind.
- Forget it.
- It's not your fault.
- It really doesn't matter at all.
- Think no more of it.
- Don't give it another thought.
- Don't take it too hard.
- I'll let you off this time.

Unit 5 Comparison and Contrast

Objectives

- Learn expressions of identifying similarities and differences
  辨识相同与不同

- Learn to describe similarities and differences between two things
  描述两者之间的相同与不同

着眼细节，精准描述。

Section 1 Getting started

Activity 1

Read each sentence below and think of one word which best fits each gap.

1. Both the top picture _____ the bottom one appear to have some kind of river in them.

2. There seem to be lots of people in this place, _____ only a few people in this one.

3. This boy looks happy. _____ contrast, the boy in the other picture appears to be disappointed or even about to cry.

4. _____ the modern scene above, the setting in the one underneath is almost certainly somewhere historic like a capital city.

5. This city road is suffering from some kind of traffic jam, and so
    _____ this highway.

6. The people in this photo are rushing somewhere, and these people
    appear to be busy _____ well.

7. These men are pretty unhappy, and these women must be _____.

8. A difference between the two photographs which stands _____ is
    the amount of green.

9. One thing that the two scenes have _____ common is what looks
    like some kind of celebration.

10. One of the few similarities _____ the two places shown is that
    there are slopes, maybe hills or mountains.

11. Another similarity _____ is instantly apparent is the presence of
    animals.

12. _____ most obvious similarity for me is the look of happiness
    on the people's faces.

13. _____ important difference between the two pictures is the
    country they are in, with this one obviously somewhere in northern
    Europe but this one probably in Africa.

14. The buildings in the two photos are really quite similar. _____
    example, they are both made from some kind of stone or perhaps
    brick.

15. The places in the pictures are fairly different _____ terms of
    what people are doing there.

16. The atmospheres are pretty different _____ that I get an excited
    feeling from this scene but this one seems quite calm.

17. The activities don't _____ much in common, but I suppose you could get paid for both of them.

18. I'd say that there are more similarities _____ differences between them.

19. One contrast _____ the sports is how exciting they probably are.

20. The only similarity between the two kinds of transport _____ I can see is ….

21. _____ main similarity between the two classrooms is….

22. I reckon quite _____ lot more water is being used here than in this place.

Activity 2

Categorize the words or expressions in the list below into the groups in which all expressions mean exactly the same.

absolutely identical	almost completely different	almost exactly the same
almost identical	almost the same	antonyms
basically the same	complete opposites	completely different
don't have much in common	exact synonyms	exactly the same
have a lot in common	have little in common	have much in common
have nothing in common	have one similarity	have quite a lot in common
have some similarities	have something in common	have things in common

have very little in common	nearly the same	only slightly different
only very slightly different	practically synonyms	rather similar
share one feature	share some features	totally different
very different	very nearly the same	very similar
virtually identical		

Activity 3

Read the following situation and choose appropriate sentences to complete the dialogue. Then act it out with your partner.

(Setting: Todd and Mark work at the same company. They are talking about similarities and differences between Americans and Canadians.)

T: OK, Mike, I was wondering, you're from Canada, and you have lived in America, and we work together, and in our company everybody is American but you, so _____?

M: Well, to be honest, just to start, I'll say that _____
_____,
I mean, I think Canadians have a lot more in common with Americans than they do, with even with English people who are like from Britain who were the original sort of Canadians, I suppose, a few hundred years ago, so in that way I think that like again, just to preempt (取代，先发制人) it by saying we're very similar. However, _____
_____.
First of all, I think Canadians in general are maybe a little bit more humble. Not to put this in a negative way, _____
_____

who'll want to debate and get to the bottom of a topic. I'm feeling pretty confident about it. _____

and say, you know, "That's, you're right. That's fine, great" but again, and I can't speak for all Canadians because it depends on your personality too, but _____.

Also, I would say that _____,

just in the way they, I guess, view, relations, or view discussionswith people, but _____,

again, I'll preempt that by saying all of the Americans that I work with are quite liberal and not conservative thinking at all, but if you want to generalize, yeah, culturally, then I think _____

_____, or people in the cultures.

T: Yeah, anything else, any other differences?

M: Well, I think, one thing that Americans tend to point to with Canadians, and _____, other than our love of hockey, is sense of humor. I think Canadians in general tend to have. I wouldn't say unique, but they just tend to look at I guess, look at things with a little bit more of humor, to it, and I think the main reason for that is cause it's so bloody cold in Canada.

T: Fair enough. Thanks Mike.

Options:

1. Canadians would rather just sort of back off	3. there're definitely some differences between Americans and Canadians
2. Americans in general tend to be a lot more businesslike and maybe even a little more conservative	4. how would you say Canadians are different than Americans

5. just to generalize, that's one difference	8. it is true to some extent
6. Canadians and Americans share a lot more similar qualities than they do differences	9. they're not as willing to engage in an argument, or to argue over a point, as most of my American friends
7. those are probably a couple of differences between the two cultures	10. Canadians tend to be a little bit more liberal, a little bit more free and easy-going

如何构架两者异同对比的描述。

Section II Let's talk

 Activity 1

Look at the two pictures below and describe each with your partner by answering questions like "Who are they?" "What are they doing?" etc. Then compare them by using the language like "The first picture shows... but the second..." and "The main difference is...".

Activity 2

Work in pairs to compare the most important festival in western culture and Chinese culture by completing the chart below. Then make a conversation in which one talks about Christmas while the other talks about the Spring Festival, using appropriate expressions to indicate similarities and differences between the two.

Differences	Christmas	The Spring Festival
DATES & DURATION	- always on December 25th - lasts two weeks, from December 24th until January 6th, the Epiphany	- _____ _____ - _____ _____
ORIGIN	- a religious holiday linked to the Catholic religion - Jesus Christ's birth	- pagan roots, linked to the rural life - an ancient legend about a monster Nian being banished by using red-color objects and loud noises, which frightened him
DECORATION	- streets, the shops and homes with lights and Christmas trees - the typical colors red and gold	- decorated as well, the typical decorations: red paper cut out and nodes with red thread - _____ _____
FOOD	- each region has its own dishes, but typical food include turkey, nuts, sweets and cakes - in general all the reunions are related to food and drinks	- also celebrated around the table eating together - typical foods such as fish and dumplings representing wealth and prosperity because of their name or appearance for their symbolic meaning

RITES	celebrated with the community the birth of Jesus Christ by the Christmas Holy Mass, usually at midnight December 24 or 25 in the morning	welcomed with lion and dragon dances in a parade through the streets of the city
GIFTS	- time for gift change - children for Santa Claus to bring them presents - adults exchange different kinds of gifts, often food or drink or sometimes even money	- gift exchange also typical - _____ _____ - adults exchange gifts as fruit baskets, sweets, alcohol, tea etc.
GAMES & SPECIAL EVENTS	- Christmas carols, parties - after eating, play games as bingo or cards	- fireworks & firecrackers - _____ _____
FAMILY HOLIDAY	- family reunion, a time when you meet the extended family, with grandparents, uncles, cousins to celebrate all together.	- _____ _____ _____ _____

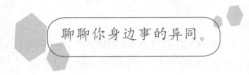

聊聊你身边事的异同。

Section III Comprehensive work

 Activity 1

Listen to a conversation between two friends. Then work in groups to talk about your hometown respectively. Take turns to compare your hometowns in terms of population, life pace, cost of living, construction, traffic and environment, etc. Finally discuss the advantages and disadvantages of city life and country life.

Activity 2

Work in a group to discuss the dilemma concerning your future plan: would you like to find a job or pursue a higher degree after finishing undergraduate studies? Why? Some useful expressions are given below.

➤ useful experience that cannot get from books

➤ give full play to the practical abilities

➤ be promoted to a higher position

➤ knowledge is power

➤ knowledge improve overall character

➤ in the long run

你还可以这样说！

Language Focus

Comparing 比较相同／相似

- Similarly / Likewise / In the same way, …
- … the same …
- … the same as …
- … also ...
- …, too.
- Both A and B …
- A is similar to B in that (they) …
- A and B are similar in that (they) …
- Like A, B [verb]…
- Compared with A, B [verb] …
- One way in which …
- It seems similar to …

Contrasting 对比不同

- However / In contrast / By contrast, …
- …, but / yet …
- On the other hand / Nevertheless, …
- while / whereas / even though / although [sentence]
- Unlike A, B [verb]…

Unit 6 Agreement and Disagreement

 Objectives

- Learn expressions of agreement and disagreement
  表达赞同和不赞同

- Learn to give reasons for agreement / disagreement
  解释为何赞同 / 不赞同

- Learn to show agreement / disagreement in discussion
  在讨论过程中表达赞同 / 不赞同

表达赞同 / 不赞同。

Section I Getting started

Activity 1

Read the following two statements and show your attitude. Give your reasons.

My attitude/My reasons	Agree /Reason	Partially agree / Reason	Disagree / Reason
Statement 1: Students should take a part-time job to enrich their experience.			
Statement 2: A successful student should be ambitious.			

Activity 2 🎧

Listen to the conversation and choose appropriate sentences to complete the dialogue.

(Setting: David and Jerry are watching a football match on TV. While doing this, they're chatting about the ball games and expressing their opinions about football.)

D: Well, no one can resist the temptation of soccer, it's really fantastic.

J: Mm, could be. _____.

D: Football has been a part of modern civilization. I'd like to say that soccer is the most exciting sport.

J: _____, but a lot of games are very exciting. I love basketball. Michael Jordan, what a great name! Although he has retired, the Chicago Bulls as well as the NBA will live with me forever.

D: So you're a diehard (顽固的，死硬的) basketball fan?

J: _____. You are a good football player?

D: No, but I like playing football. I play every day and always watch matched on television.

J: I hate watching football games, it's slow and so few goals are scored in ninety minutes.

D: _____. Your weird opinion surprised me very much. Football is the most popular sport in the world. Every football player might become a world-renown star.

J: _____. Tennis isn't less popular than football.

D: Maybe, but you know The World Cup is for football.

J: OK, _____.

Options:

1. I'm not sure I can agree	6. Oh, I don't know
2. Absolutely	7. You're kidding
3. You must like football very much	8. I'll say
4. But you carry it too far, don't you	9. That's just what I think, of course
5. Let's agree to disagree	10. I see what you mean

Activity 3

Read the following conversation and act them out with your partner.

L: Well, Xiao Ming, I think sport is good for you and everybody should take exercise.

X: I quite agree, Li Ping.

L: Too many students sit in their classrooms all day. They don't get out and do anything to keep fit.

X: You're absolutely right.

L: I love football. I play it every week and always watch the matches on television. I think we should have more football matches on TV.

X: Oh, I'm not so sure about that. There's usually one football match every week. I think that's quite enough.

L: I don't think one football match every week is enough. I think there should be far more matches, three or four at least!

X: I'm afraid I totally disagree with you. Maybe there should be more sports on TV, but different things, too. Table tennis is very exciting to watch.

L: Well, let's agree to disagree.

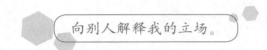

向别人解释我的立场。

Section II   Let's talk

Activity 1

Work in pairs. Follow the model and discuss whether young people should still rely on their parents' financial help after they graduate and get a job.

Model:

A: Many young people today still rely on their parents' financial help after they've got jobs. What do you think of the phenomenon?

B: If you ask me, I think it is shameful.

A: Maybe, but don't you think family members should help each other?

B: That's not exactly what I mean. Of course, they could help each other in case of emergency. But I think young people should try to live within their means once they graduate and get a job to support themselves.

Activity 2

Work in pairs. One of you starts a conversation by choosing one of the following viewpoints and then supplies an example to exemplify your point. Your partner will agree partly, add something to your point and give examples to support his / her opinion. You may take turns to imitate the conversation.

Model:

A: Animals communicate with one another by means of cries.

B: You think so?

A: Yes, for example, cats find mates by crying.

B: Well, that's true, but animals also communicate by other means.

A: Such as?

B: Such as by physical contact, smell, color, etc.

Viewpoint	Example	Counterargument	Counterexample
Cell phone is very important in our life.	People can communicate anytime and anywhere with cell phone.	Cell phone disturbs our life.	Young people depend on it too much.
Celebrating Christmas is very popular in China now.	It's a usual way of spending leisure time.	It is totally useless for Chinese to celebrate Christmas.	Chinese traditional festivals, such as Spring Festival will be influenced a lot.
Shopping online is more convenient and time-saving.	We can almost buy anything online.	Shopping online may lure us into debts.	We may be tempted or fooled into buying things we do not need or thing of little value.

Activity 3

Discuss with your partner about following statements. Show your agreement and disagreement and give reasons.

1. It is impolite to make some sound when eating.

2. It is quite common and all right that a group of people chat loudly in restaurant.

3. It should be banned that people step on the lawn in the public place.

4. It is understandable that the visitors take pictures in the museum.

5. It doesn't matter to write down something on the book borrowed from the library.

在讨论中恰当的表达立场。

Section III Comprehensive work

Activity 1

You are having a dinner with your friends. Discuss with them about the menu. Show your agreements and disagreements and give your reasons.

≡ DINNER ≡
MENU
AVAILABLE 5-9PM

SNACKS & BURGERS

Skinny Fries *with* Aioli	$7.00
Stone &Wood Battered Onion Rings *with* Tomato Relish	$7.00
Vegetarian Spring Rolls *with* Sweet Chilli Sauce	$7.50
Wedges *with* Sweet Chilli and Sour Cream	$8.00
Vegetarian Nachos	$10.00
Beef Nachos	$12.00
Chicken BLT on Turkish *with* Fries	$11.00
Beef,Cheese and Slaw Burger on a Brioche Bun *with* Fries	$13.00

MAIN MEALS

Chicken Katsu *with* Rice	$12.00
Quinoa, Roast Pumpkin and Feta Salad (V)	$13.00
add Chicken or Prawns	$3.00
Chicken Schnitzel *with* Salad and Fries	$13.50
Chicken Parmigiana *with* Salad and Fries	$14.5
Rump Steak *with* Salad and Fries *choose* Gravy,Creamy Mushroom or Pepper Sauce	$15.50

All fries served *with* aioli. Please ask our staff about further dietary options or substitutions.

WEDNESDAY	THURSDAY	FRIDAY	SATURDAY
double deal 2X CHICKEN SCHNITZELS W/ SALAD & FRIES $16	300g RUMP STEAK W/ SALAD & FRIES + $18	*Parmy* & PALE ALE CHICKEN PARMY W/ SALAD & FRIES + $16	*double deal* 2x BEEF, CHEESE & SLAW BURGERS W/ FRIES $16

kerbside

Activity 2

Your plane crashed in the middle of a desert in Mexico and the pilot died on the spot. Before the crash, the pilot sent signals to ask for secure. Two of the passengers are severely injured. From the map, you know that 300 miles away, there is a military station. The temperature in desert during daytime can reach 100 centigrade and below zero at night. You all wear light clothes. Now discuss with your group members and choose 4 items from the following things to make sure you can survive. Show your agreements or disagreements during the discussion and give your reasons.

➤ A white-and-red parachute

➤ A knife

➤ A bottle of salt tablets

➤ Machine to measure blood

➤ Flashlight

➤ Compass

➤ A map of the desert

➤ A book to tell what are eatable in desert

➤ Water for 4 days

➤ Thick clothes

➤ A pistol

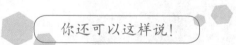

你还可以这样说！

Language Focus

Entire Agreement

- Absolutely! / Exactly! / Definitely!
- That's absolutely true.
- That's for sure.
- That's no doubt about it.
- That's exactly my opinion.
- You hit the nail on the head.

- I couldn't have said it better.
- I think I'd go along with you there.
- I share your view on that.
- I couldn't have said it better myself.

Partial agreement

- Could be, but you go to the extreme.
- Mm. Maybe you are right.
- I don't entirely agree with you.
- Yes, in a way, but…
- That's worth thinking about.
- I see your point, but we still had better …
- There's something in that, I suppose.
- There is a lot in your opinion, but something was ignored.
- Yes. I agree up to a point.

Indirect disagreement

- Do you think so?
- But I think in a different way.
- I'm afraid I don't see it that way.
- Well, I'm not really sure.
- Mm, I'm not sure I can agree.
- I'm inclined to disagree with that.
- All right, let's agree to disagree.
- That really surprises me. I wonder if there are some mistakes.
- Well, I don't know. But don't you think that …?

Direct disagreement

- Not really.
- I entirely disagree with you.
- I'm afraid you are wrong there.
- You've got it all wrong.
- You don't know what you are talking about.
- You can't expect me to believe that.
- I don't see eye to eye with you.
- I won't listen to any more of this crap (废话).

Unit 7 Invitation

Objectives

- Learn expressions of offering invitations 提出邀请

- Learn to accept or decline invitations
  接受／拒绝他人的邀请

- Learn to give reasons when declining invitations
  礼貌地拒绝邀请并给出解释

怎样向别人提出邀请。

Section I Getting started

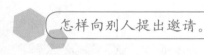

Match the following invitations with possible responds.

- Would you like to see a movie with me this weekend?

- Could you come to my birthday party tomorrow evening?

- May I invite you to attend a painting exhibition?

- I'll be glad if you can come to the spring outing with us.

- Well, I have to finish my English paper tonight.

- Oh, I'd like to. But I have no idea of painting.

- Great! Where are we going to?

- Mm, I heard it is very expensive there.

- Are you free tonight?

- I was thinking of taking a dinner in the new buffet. Do you want to come?

- Have you made any plans for the summer holidays?

- Shall we go shopping tonight?

- Oh, I haven't decided. But I really want to go to the seaside.

- Sorry! I've got an appointment with John.

- Sure. I will buy you a surprise gift!

- Sound interesting. What's the name of the movie?

Activity 2

Now imagine you are inviting your partner to the following famous tourist attractions.

 Activity 3

Listen to the conversation, and then choose appropriate sentences to complete the dialogue.

(Setting: Lily is inviting Beth to a National Day party.)

L: Hi, Beth. I've been thinking of asking you _____

_____.

B: No, not really.

L: Well, _____.

B: Sure, _____. Who are you inviting?

L: Some young teachers from the department and three of your American students. That way you can practice your Chinese, too.

B: That's a great idea. What can I bring?

L: Let's see. I'll practice everything Chinese, and …

B: Why don't I make a potato salad?

L: _____.

B: Is there any way I can help?

L: Well, I should let them know about the party, so they won't plan anything else.

B: Right. I'll be seeing Bob and Jane tomorrow. Do you want me to tell them about it?

L: Oh, please.

B: _____?

L: About five. I'd like everyone to come early so that you can talk before dinner. Oh, and one more thing, could you ask Bob to bring his records?

B: _____.

L: Thanks. Bye-bye.

B: Bye.

Options:

1. I'll pick you up	6. Sure thing
2. That's terrific	7. What time do you want them to show up
3. Could we make it some other time then	8. I' like to come
4. I'm afraid I can't	9. if you have any plans for the Chinese National Day
5. I was planning to have a party at my house	10. Oh, that's too bad

接受／拒绝别人的邀请

Section II   Let's talk

Activity 1

Work with your partner and complete the flowing conversations.

(Conversation 1: Anne is inviting her friend Jim over for her birthday party.)

Anne: I will hold my birthday party tonight. We are having a little get-together at my place. _____.

Jim: _____. When do you want me to be there?

Anne: 7:00?

Jim: _____.

Anne: _____.

(Conversation 2: Sam is inviting his colleague Tom for a drink.)

Sam: How about a drink tonight?

Tom: _____. I have an appointment with my classmates. _____.

Sam: Oh, that's OK! Have a good night.

Tom: You too!

(Conversation 3: Jenny is inviting her boss, Mr. Brown, for a dinner.)

Jan: Good morning, Mr. Brown. _____?

Brown: _____.

Jan: Good!

Brown: _____.

Jan: _____.

Brown: OK. See you at 6:00 then.

Activity 2

Mike invites John to go to a basketball game but John has no interest in it. John invites Mike to see a movie together and he agrees. Mike suggests the time and place to meet and they agree on the movie they are going to see.

M: Greets and invites J.

J: Declines the invitation and gives the reason.

M: Expresses his disappointment.

J: Invites M to go to see a movie.

M: Accepts the invitation with pleasure.

M: Suggests the time and the place to meet.

J: Agrees, confirms exact location.

M: Asks about the movie.

J: Suggests the movie they are going to see.

M: Agrees. Anticipates meeting B later.

拒绝他人的邀请并解释原因。

Section III   Comprehensive work

Activity 1 : The Farewell Party!

You are going to hold a farewell party since it is the last week in your college. Work in group of four and discuss the following items of your party.

1. Make an invitation card.

2. Discuss the exact details of the party, such as: date and time, place, presenter and participants, party processes.

3. Walk around the classroom and invite classmates form other group to your party. Give him a card if he accepts the invitation.

4. Find out which group has send out most invitation cards.

Activity 2 : A Hope Primary School

Work in groups of 7. You are a principle appointed to set up a new Hope Primary School in a remoted town of Central China, where no school has existed before, for about 60 children ranging in age from 7 to 16. Now you are going to invite the following candidates to help you to set up the school. One student acts as the principle, inviting other students and other students act as the candidates.

Candidate 1: An older teacher, experienced, wise, but rather skeptical.

Candidate 2: A young teacher fresh from university, town-bred and out of touch with local conditions.

Candidate 3: The village head, eager for his village to have the school, willing to help.

Candidate 4: A young woman from the village, mother of prospective pupils, uneducated but eager to be involved.

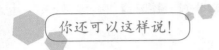

你还可以这样说！

Language Focus

Extending invitations

- Would you like to / care to/ be interested in…?
- How would you like to …?
- Would you free to …?
- Could you please come to …?
- What are you up to today?
- Do you have any plans for tonight?
- Do you feel like to …?
- May I invite you to …?
- Shall we have … tonight?
- Are you free tonight?

- I'll be glad if you can come to …
- I'd like to invite you to…
- I do hope you can …
- I was wondering if you were doing anything.
- I was wondering if you would like to …
- I was thinking of …. Do you want to come?
- … You will come, will you?

- Have you made any plans?
- May we have the pleasure of your presence at the meeting?
- Would you honor us with …?
- If you could manage, we'd like you to…
- Perhaps you'd care to …

Accepting invitations

- Good idea!
- With pleasure.
- All right then.
- Sounds great!
- You bet!
- I'm on! Thanks very much.
- I'm most grateful!
- I'd like nothing better than …
- I won't say no.
- I'll take you up on that.
- Great! I'll count on it.
- Yea, that would be nice.
- Sure, I'd like to/ love to / pleased to.

- Thanks. I will if I can.
- Sure, why not? / That would be.
- Yes. How nice of you!
- Why don't we!

- We'd like to accept your invitation.
- What a splendid idea! Thank you.
- That would give us great pleasure.
- Thank you for your kind invitation to …

Declining invitations

- That would be nice, but I'm afraid I'm rather tied up.
- That's very kind of you, but I can't manage it.
- That's very kind of you, but I've already arranged to / promised to…
- Sorry! I've got a previous appointment.
- Well, I'd like to, but I'm not sure I have time.
- Well, as a matter of fact, I had planned to…
- Thank you. But I'm afraid I have other appointment.
- Thanks for asking, but I'm busy now. Sorry!
- I'm sorry, but I've got another engagement.
- I'm afraid I can't, but thanks anyway.
- I'm afraid I can't come. I'm going to…
- I wish I could, but you see I …

- I wish I could, but I'm busy. Maybe another time, though.
- I would love to any other time, but I've already made plans.
- I would like very much to go, but I have to…
- I hate to turn you down, but I must…

- I appreciate the invitation, but I'm afraid I can't.
- Sorry, I'm not sure if I can.
- If you don't mind, I'd rather not.
- Oh, dear! What a pity. I'm going to…
- Not really, thanks all the same. You see I've promised to…
- What about a rain check?
- Maybe next time.

- Much as I should like to, I'm afraid I'm already booked up …
- Much to my regret, I wouldn't be able to… with you.
- Sadly on that particular day I shall… . However, thank you for thinking of me.

- Unfortunately, I'll have to… that day.
- It's unlucky we'll be back before the date you suggested.
- It's regretted we are unable to accept your invitation.
- I regret that a prior engagement prevents me from accepting your kind invitation.

Unit 8 Describing a person / an event or an experience

Objectives

- Learn expressions of describing a person, an event or an experience
  描述一个人，一件事或一次经历

- Learn to describe a person's physical appearance and personalities
  描绘人物的外貌及性格

- Learn to describe an event or an experience in a proper order
  按照合适的顺序描述事件或经历

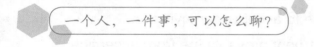

一个人，一件事，可以怎么聊？

Section I Getting started

Examine the following portraits of Mona Lisa and identify the distinctive facial features in each of them by choosing the relevant vocabulary in the list below.

For example: Mona Lisa A has straight hair parted in the middle.

straight hair parted in the middle   bald

moustache on the upper lip   bang

Afro hair   chubby   big cheekbones

thick lips   dark-skinned   fusiform eyes

straight nose   curly hair   smiling lips

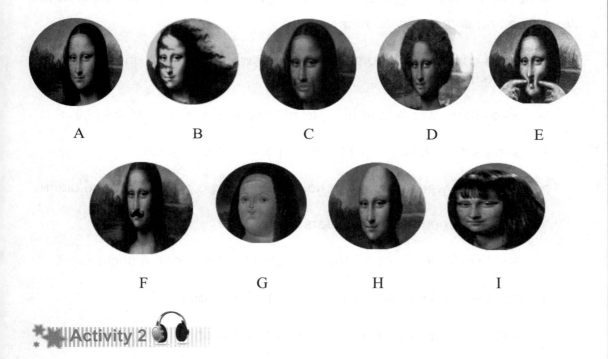

A   B   C   D   E

F   G   H   I

Activity 2

Listen to a conversation between a man and a woman talking about their kids and themselves. Identify the personalities of each one mentioned.

Person	Personalities
younger son of the man	
older son of the man	
the woman	

the sister of the woman	
the man	

Activity 3

Read the following segments and arrange them in the correct order of the story. Then retell the story to your partner.

➤ I was coming back home from Turkey where I'd been on holiday with some friends

➤ when there was a loud bang from the right hand side of the plane

➤ and said there was a problem with one of the engines

➤ we had to wait for about an hour, and then we got back on the plane

➤ this happened about five years ago

➤ and I could see a lot of smoke coming from one of the engines

➤ anyway, we were on the plane and had just taken off

➤ and then a few minutes later the pilot came on

➤ and we'd have to return to the airport

➤ about ten minutes later we landed without any problems

➤ of course, everyone started looking around but the plane carried on flying normally

➤ actually it was a different plane, and I was pretty relieved that it was

从一个人的外貌谈起……

Section II Let's talk

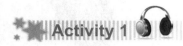

Complete the following dialogue with the appropriate sentences and then act it out with your partner.

(Setting: Maggie is going to get a part-time job and she is talking to her friend Joe on the phone to get some information about her future boss Alex Wilson.)

M: Hi, Joe, this is Maggie, Maggie Graham.

J: Oh, hi, Maggie. How are you?

M: I'm fine. How are you?

J: Fine.

M: Listen, um… _____

— You know him, don't you?

J: Sure.

M: _____?

J: Well, why are you asking about Alex?

M: Well, I want to try and get a part time job at his store …

J: Oh, well, Alex's nice guy …

M: Mm-hmm.

J: I mean _____.

M: Well, that sounds good. Um, _____?
I've got to meet him at the Sunset restaurant for lunch and I can't remember.

J: Oh, well he's about mid-thirty.

M: Uh-huh.

J: … six-foot-two…

M: Right.

J: … Oh, _____.

M: Oh, sounds kind of handsome.

J: Mm.

M: Um, is he a formal kind of guy, or does he dress casually?

J: Oh, he rarely dresses casually. _____
— dresses very much in style.

M: Oh, I see, I better dress up then … OK, thanks a lot. Bye!

J: Bye! Have a good time!

Options:

1. he's well-built, mature and speaks with magnetic voice	4. what's he like
2. that was scary	5. I want to ask you some questions about Alex Wilson
3. he always wears three-piece suits and ties	6. he looks helpful, but I don't think he means it

7. his hair is brown	9. he's got a square face and a flat nose
8. what does he look like	10. he'll give you decent hours, a decent pay, and plenty of breaks

Activity 2

Work with your partner to play the role of a boss and an employee who is asked to meet the newly appointed project director at the airport this afternoon at four. Make a dialogue with words or phrases provided below to talk about some information concerning him.

> in his early forties   short but stout   moustache
>
> short brown hair   black suit and yellow tie

Activity 3

Interview as many different partners as possible, asking and answering the questions and completing the worksheet below. Then give feedback to the rest of the class on what you have found about your classmates with any interesting examples and description.

Find someone who…	Name	Example
… likes to try new and exciting things.		
… has a lot of energy and is very active.		
… is always accidentally breaking or hitting things.		
… treats everyone equally and in a reasonable way.		
… is determined to be successful, rich or famous.		
… is worried about something.		
… is always working very hard.		
… easily understands feelings of other people.		
… likes to tell other people what to do.		
… makes choices and decides what to do quickly and confidently.		
… is relaxed, calm, and easy to get along with.		
… always to find out about something.		
… makes other people laugh.		
… shows good manners and respect for other people.		
… is confident and not afraid of people.		
… is careful to avoid problems and danger.		

一起来讲故事吧！

Section　III　Comprehensive work

Activity 1

There was a robbery at a bank this morning. You happened to see the robber and the whole process. Work in groups and take turns to play the role of the witness who describes the robber & robbery and the role of the policeman who draws a "mug shot" and takes some notes based on the description. Then discuss these mug shots and notes in your group to find out who's made the clearest description and the most similar one to the witness's depiction.

- When? _____
- Where? _____
- What happened? _____
- Number of people injured: _____
- Type of injuries: _____
- Was any first aid given? _____
- Where did the robber go? _____

Activity 2

Work in groups to create a story about an exciting or unforgettable event or experience. Each member of the group take turns to contribute one sentence in the story by using connecting phrases such as " to start out, first, after that, the next thing, in the middle of, before, finally, in the end ". Then work with a partner from a different group to tell your story. Finally, retell your partner's story.

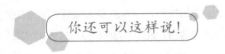

你还可以这样说!

Language Focus

Describing a person 描绘一个人

- What's he / she like?
- What does he / she look like?
- What do you think of …?
- What does he / she do?
- What's his / her hobby?
- What's the color of …'s eyes / hair?
- What happened to …?
- Can you recognize … in the crowd?
- Could you tell me how … looks like?
- Could you describe his / her appearance?
- Do you know who … is?
- Have you seen … lately
- Is he / she popular with…?

- Judging from his / her look … is a very … man.
- Judging from his / her appearance, … must be …
- I think I have a pretty good idea as to how he / she looks.
- I think I have a good picture of how he / she looks.
- I think I can figure out how he / she looks.
- I think I wouldn't have any difficulty in recognizing him / her.

- He / she has a … nose / complexion / figure / look.
- He / she has got … hair.
- He / she is … inches tall.
- He / she looks / appears / seems …
- He / she is good-looking / plain-looking / ugly.
- He / she looks old / young for his / her age.
- He / she is a bag of bones.
- His / her voice is …
- He / she always likes to wear … clothes / ties / hat / shoes.
- She wears … make-up.
- The man / woman in … (color) is …
- He / she is a very … person.
- He / she has a very … nature.
- He seems like … guy.
- He / she is always in trouble.
- He / she is kind of …
- He / she comes from …
- He / she likes / doesn't like …

Describing an Event / Experience 描述一件事／一次经历

- How is everything going?
- Was everything OK?
- Did you enjoy …?
- How was your …?
- How did it go?

- Guess what!
- Ask me what just happened.
- You know what!
- You're not going to believe what happened.
- You'll never guess …
- You won't believe …
- Here's what happened.
- I hate to talk about it.
- What were you doing when … happened?
- What happened next?
- What did you think at that time?
- What did you do after that?
- What have you been doing since I saw you last time?
- What would you have done if you hadn't …?
- How did it happen?
- How do you know about it?
- How did you feel when it broke out?
- Have you ever …?
- Do you still remember what you did when the accident happened?
- Did you experience that event?
- Did you think of calling for help?

- Were you … (feeling) at that time?

- Looking back on it, I think I shouldn't have …
- Had I …, I wouldn't have …
- I hurried to…
- I used to …
- I would have … if I had …
- I wish I had …
- I had thought about … but I didn't …
- You should have …
- It has been a long time since …
- … had messed up all our plans.
- Everything happened so fast that I don't think I can recognize …
- You would too if you'd been through / experienced what I have.
- It took me quite a while / a long time to …
- That still wasn't the end of my troubles.
- That was not at all the end of all my problems.
- The worst of it wasn't over yet.
- That was the … time that I had …

- First of all / To begin with / first, I thought …
- Subsequently / Later / Then I realized …
- While … , / Simultaneously / At the same time we found …
- The next thing I did was to …
- Finally, I decided …
- In the end, …

Unit 9　Problems and Solutions

Objectives

- Learn expressions of talking about problems 讨论问题

- Learn to ask someone for his/her problems 询问问题

- Learn to provide solutions and give suggestions 提供建议解决问题

拆穿人生艰难之麻烦多多。

Section I　Getting started

Activity 1

Look at a list of top 10 most annoying problems in modern life according to a poll of 2,000 Britons for Nurofen Express and think of the top 5 of yours. Ask for advice from your partner to deal with them.

➤ Your laptop/computer freezing

➤ Nuisance calls

➤ Slow Wi-Fi

➤ Being stuck in traffic

➤ People who take up two parking spaces

➢ Public transport delays

➢ Spam email

➢ When people throw their rubbish out of the car window

➢ The rising cost of living

➢ When people let their children misbehave in restaurants

 **Activity 2**

Listen to a news clip about fighting colds and fill in blanks with the information learned from it. Then summarize the ways to protect yourself from colds or flu in your own words.

It's easy to spread germs that cause colds, flu and other illnesses. According to the US centers for disease control and prevention, this is why you need to protect yourself and _____. The agency recently published a list of recommendations to stay healthy. It advises to _____with people who are sick. If you are sick, stay home. When you cough or sneeze, _____with a tissue. Frequently wash your hands. Avoid _____. Clean and disinfect often-used surfaces at home, work or school. Get plenty of sleep and _____. Drink plenty of nonalcoholic fluids to stay well-hydrated. Finally, maintain _____.

 **Activity 3**

Complete the following dialogue with the appropriate sentences and then act it out with your partner.

(Setting: Michael is quitting smoking and has tried many ways. He is talking to Lisa who is giving some advice.)

L: This is it. I'm quitting smoking for good.

M: Good for you. Are you going cold turkey?

L: No, _____. I craved cigarettes too much.

M: _____? Have you tried that?

L: Yes, but I didn't like the side effects. It irritated my throat.

M: That's too bad. _____?

L: Yes, I have. I became addicted to (对······有瘾) the patches and couldn't wean (使丢弃) myself off of them. _____.

M: And electronic cigarettes?

L: They only made me want to smoke a real cigarette. _____

_____.

M: So, what now?

L: I'm going to try hypnosis. I hear that it works for some people.

M: And _____?

L: _____. Some people say that's effective

for quitting smoking.

M: _____. Sometimes the cure is truly worse than the disease!

Options:

1. they were no help at all	5. I suppose you've tried nicotine patches, too
2. if that doesn't work	6. I just traded one addiction for another
3. the last resort is acupuncture	7. how about nicotine gum
4. I tried that, but it didn't work	8. if you say so

贡献你的生活智慧。

Section II Let's talk

Make a dialogue with your partner based on the following scenarios.

1. The city is going to pass a law against walking dogs on the street. Discuss the pros and cons of the law and some possible solutions for dog owners, such as cleaning up the dogs' mess, building a dog park, etc.

2. A reporter is interviewing a guy who used to be compulsive gambler, but has got rid of the problem now. He describes how he feels in gambling by comparing it to alcoholism and how he fights against it with the help of a doctor after having failed to stop on his own. The beginning part of the conversation is given below.

R: *Good morning, Mr. Brown. I'm a correspondent with the magazine Health. I hear you've overcome your gambling problem. First of all,* could you describe your problems in the past?

B: Yeah. I did have serious gambling problems. You can't understand gambling as an addiction till you've been hooked.

R: Could you tell me your feelings at that time?

B: There was a sensation like the one that comes with drugs or alcohol, and I just couldn't help wanting more and more.

R: …

Activity 2

Work with your partner to play the one role of two residents living in APT 102 and 202 respectively. Make a conversation to work out a solution to the problem that annoys both of you.

Resident of **APT 102**

It's 7:00 am. You are a drummer, and music major. This Friday is your senior recital. If you don't play well you can't graduate so you have to practice as much as possible.

Resident of **APT 202**

It's 7:00 am. You were up until 4:00 am preparing for an important business meeting. You have to give your presentation at 9:30, and you really need another hour or two to sleep. You can't sleep because the person who lives downstairs is playing the drums — it's not the first time this has happened.

三个臭皮匠赛过诸葛亮。

Section III Comprehensive work

Activity 1

Work in groups to discuss the environmental problems and some possible solutions in turns, following the example and using expressions listed below.

Example: Speaking of air pollution in our cities, it might be a good idea to use public transportation when travelling long distances.

➤ the best solution might be …

➤ when it comes to…

➤ one solution to …

➤ the problem as … is more likely to be solved by …

➤ it would be an effective way of …

➤ there is a strong possibility that …

➤ this would probably help to …

Problem	Solution
➤ Rivers, lakes, and oceans are becoming more polluted by large amount of chemicals and plastics dump as well as human waste and rubbish into the water. **(Water pollution)** ➤ **Environmental accidents** such as oil spills and radioactive leaks threaten wildlife and the ecosystem. ➤ Airborne materials that can lead to ozone pollution cause human health problems and damage to plants and animals. **(Ozone depletion)** ➤ Man-made chemicals released into the dirt either by accident or through poor disposal techniques cause **soil contamination.** ➤ The mishandling of **hazardous waste** materials poses immediate and long-term risks to plants, animals, humans and the environment.	➤ A. Create additional safety protocol using both computerized and human detection systems. ➤ B. Issue stringent laws against such contamination and make sure that the appropriate agencies have to be tough in the enforcement of those laws. ➤ C. Make sure that disposal experts handle all waste, and should never dump them with regular trash or into rivers or ditches. ➤ D. Avoid products from nonrenewable sources and avoid throwing stuff away if they can be reused, repaired, or recycled. ➤ E. Enforce laws controlling the release of dangerous substances into the atmosphere.

Activity 2

Study in a group the present layout of a zoo and a list of problems which need changes. Then discuss the situation and try to arrive at a new layout which will solve all the problems.

ZOO LAYOUT

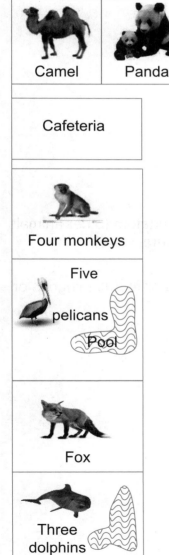

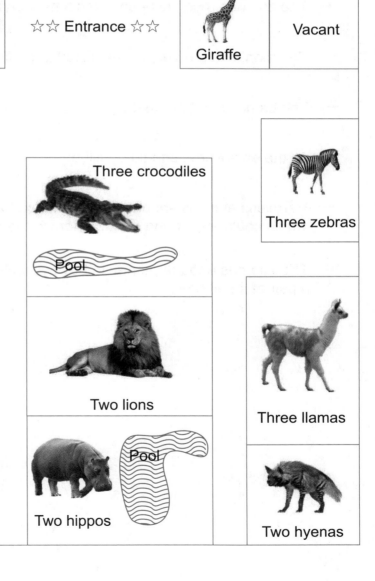

Camel	Panda
Cafeteria	
Four monkeys	
Five pelicans Pool	
Fox	
Three dolphins	

☆☆ Entrance ☆☆

| Giraffe | Vacant |

Three crocodiles

Pool

Two lions

Two hippos Pool

Three zebras

Three llamas

Two hyenas

Information for changes:

➤ The giraffe is about to give birth.

➤ One of lions has died.

➤ Small kids are alarmed by seeing the crocodiles facing them as they come in.

➤ The zoo has recently been given a new panda.

➤ The monkeys are very noisy, disturbing animals.

➤ The camel is rather smelly.

➤ All the enclosures should be filled.

➤ Harmless animals should not be put next to predators (other animals which could attack and / or eat them in the natural state).

➤ The zoo has enough money to buy two wolves or four flamingoes or a pair of small deer.

你还可以这样说！

Language Focus

Asking Someone for His / Her problem
询问某人（他／她）的问题

- What's the matter?

- What's wrong?

- What's up?

- What's the problem?

- Is anything OK / the matter / wrong?

- Is anything bothering you?

Presenting solutions / Giving advice / Suggesting
提供解决办法；提出建议

- What you could do is to …
- What would work out best is …
- Could you simply …?
- As I see it, the solution is clear to …
- Why don't you …?
- How about …?
- Why not do that / try that?
- Is there any reason why you shouldn't …?
- If I were you, I'd …
- I suggest you …
- I'd advise you to …
- I think you should / ought to / had better…
- Perhaps / Maybe you should / ought to …
- Well, it might be a good idea to …
- Well, perhaps you could … / you could consider …
- Well, you might like to try …

Unit 10　Comment on News

Objectives

- Learn expressions of giving comments 发表看法评论

- Learn to ask for opinions 询问他人观点

- Learn to express certainty, probability and possibility 表达确定及可能性

你怎么看?

Section I　Getting started

Activity 1

Read the quotes about news and decide which ones you agree with. Share your ideas with your partner.

➤　"When a dog bites a man, that is not news. But if a man bites a dog, that is news."

— John B. Bogart

➤　"News is what a chap who doesn't care much about anything wants to read. And it's only news until he's read it. After that, it's dead."

— Evelyn Waugh

➤ "News is what somebody somewhere wants to suppress; all the rest is advertising."

— Lord Northcliffe

➤ "Nothing travels faster than light, with the possible exception of bad news."

— Douglas Adams

➤ No news is good news.

— Proverb

Activity 2

Do the questionnaire. Then work in pairs and discuss your answers to the questionnaire. If none of the answer suits you, talk about your own answers.

Newspaper
1. I can't live without it!
2. I read a paper about four times a week.
3. If I see a newspaper I might pick up and read it.
4. Newspaper? Who needs newspaper?

Magazine

1. I love them — I beg, borrow or steal them whenever I can.

2. They're a great way of getting information and gossip.

3. I occasionally read magazines.

4. What a waste of time!

Radio

1. Definitely the easiest way to find out what's going on.

2. I often have the radio on when I work or study late at night.

3. I listen to the radio from time to time.

4. Who needs radio when you've got TV and the Internet?

Television

1. It's difficult to get me away from the telly, I'm afraid.

2. I watch foe maybe an hour or two each day.

3. If there's a good program on, I'll watch it.

4. TV is for old people and those who don't know how to read.

The Internet

1. If you're interested in current affairs, why use anything else?

2. I quite often read news online.

3. If I'm online, I'll sometimes look at what different papers are saying.

4. Get your news from the Internet? No, thanks!

听故事讲故事做评论！

Section II Let's talk

Activity 1

Listen to a conversation among Mark, Kate and Janet and complete the sentences.

M:	_____!
J:	What?
M:	This story I'm reading.
K:	So tell us.
M:	A man within a wheelchair crossing the road in front of a lorry at some traffic lights. Somehow, the back of the wheelchair got stuck on the front of the lorry. When the lorry started moving, it took the wheelchair and the man with it!

K:	_____!
M:	The driver drove for several miles at 80 kilometers an hour before he stopped at a garage. The man was unhurt because his seat belt had stopped him falling out.
J:	_____! Thank goodness the man was all right.
M:	The police asked the driver if he'd realized he has a passenger. The driver said he had no idea at all.
M:	Do you want to hear another one? A funny one this time.
K:	Go on.
M:	A woman reported that her car had been stolen and she'd left her mobile phone in the car. The policeman suggested calling the mobile. When he did, the thief answered it. The policeman told the thief that he was answering an ad in the paper and that he wanted to buy the car. And the thief agreed to sell it.
J:	_____.
M:	So they arranged to meet and the thief was arrested and the woman got her car back.
J:	_____!
M:	_____— I always read them.

Activity 2

Work in pairs and take turns to act out the conversation.

1. **A:** Say you read a funny news story this morning.

   B: Ask A to tell the story.

   A: Tell the first part of the story. Report what was said.

   B: Make a comment.

   A: Tell the second part of the story. Report what was said.

   B: Make a comment.

   A: Finish the story.

   B: Say what you think of the story, then ask A how he/she usually gets his / her news.

   A: Respond and then ask B the same question.

   B: Reply.

2. **A:** Think of the last TV program you watched, but don't tell B what it was.

   B: Ask A the questions below.

   - *What channel was the program on?*
   - *What time was it on?*
   - *How long was the program?*
   - *What kind of program was it?*
   - *What was it about?*
   - *What did you think of it?*
   - *Which was the best / worst part in it?*
   - *Will you watch the program nest time?*

   A: Answer the questions.

   B: Guess the name of the program.

   A: Tell B if he / she got the name right.

   B: Say what you have learned about the program and A's opinion of it.

   A: Add more information about the program.

Activity 3

According to China's Ministry of Civil Affairs, by the end of 2015, the number of single young people has reached 20 million. Comment on this news with your partner: Is being single becoming an acceptable way of life? What do you think about being single? Some people's opinions are listed below for reference.

vlwow (China)

This is a personal choice. If somebody wants to be single, then they can remain single. One thing which needs to be considered is that if you decide to be single, tell it to your parents or others who care about you, tell them truthfully your thoughts, why you have made that choice, so that they won't worry about you.

St_George (UK)

Not everybody can live on their own; in fact I would say most people can't. Even when a marriage or a relationship goes wrong and you fall out of love. You're bound to have an emotional attachment to somebody you've lived with for a long time. Lots of people don't want to grow old alone and dread the thought of dying on their own but one has to go first and the other ends up alone anyway.

DMZappa (US)

I didn't get married till I was 45. I enjoyed it and was never lonely, maybe bored at times. I watched my friends go through it all and said no thanks. I can't name one couple from back then that are still together to this day. People asked me why I never married. I just told them I never had a gal ask me.

Exportedkiwi (New Zealand)

It seems that too many young folks in China are pressured into marriages they're neither prepared for emotionally or mentally, nor are they prepared for it materially. This tradition must stop. People should be free to marry in their own time and for their own reasons, not just because society expects it when they reach a certain age. I'm in my 40's and never married and no hurry to do it either. I've seen marriages in my family, and among friends ruined because of rushing into it. I prefer to learn from others mistakes and hopefully, not make the same one(s) they do.

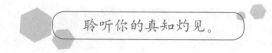

聆听你的真知灼见。

Section III Comprehensive work

Activity 1

Work in groups and prepare a short news bulletin for radio.

➤ Make a list of current news stories.

➤ Choose four or five to include in your bulletin. Two or three should be important and one or two should be amusing but unimportant.

➤ Discuss these events and share your views on the importance of keeping up to date about news and whether you believe everything you hear on the news or read in the Internet?

Activity 2

Look at the cartoons and discuss the questions below, commenting on the present social trends.

1. How would life be different without the Internet?

2. What are the pros and cons（利弊）of using Internet in our daily life?

3. Do you think the advantages of the Internet outweigh the problems associated with it?

We usually shop in the comfort of our own home but the bloody computer crashed .

"Nurse, get on the internet, go to SURGERY .COM, scroll down and click on the 'Are you totally lost ?' icon."

I'm never having kids. I hear they take nine months to download.

"You should check your e-mails more often. I fired you over three weeks ago."

你还可以这样说！

Language Focus

Asking for Opinions 询问观点

- What do you think?
- What's your opinion?
- What are your ideas?
- Do you have any thoughts on that?
- How do you feel about it?

Giving Opinions 发表看法观点

- In my opinion / view / reckoning, …
- Well, if you ask me, …
- My feeling is that …
- I (don't) think / feel / believe that…
- I strongly / genuinely / really / definitely think that …

Expressing Certainty 表达肯定观点

- Actually / Clearly / Surely / In fact / As a matter of fact, …
- Without doubt / Undoubtedly, …

Expressing Probability and Possibility 表达可能性

- I expect / doubt / guess / suppose that …
- I doubt whether …
- That's bound to …
- It's probable that …
- It's (un)likely that …
- It's doubtful whether …
- There seems to be a general acceptance that ...

Listening Scripts

Unit 1　Likes and DIslikes

Section I, Activity 2

J:　Mary! What a surprise to see you here.

M: Small world! Long time no see.

J:　Yeah, what have you been doing? I haven't heard anything about you since I saw you last year at the graduation party.

M:　Really? But I have heard a lot about you. I heard you've found a good paying job, haven't you?

J:　You're well informed.

M: I'm interested in knowing what you are thinking of that job.

J:　To be honest, *it's boring, I can't stand it.*

M: Can't you? *I'd prefer a job which can better my income.* Don't you think money is an important factor which determines our choices of a job?

J:　*Maybe lots of people are rather keen on money.* But I hate earning money without using the knowledge I learned. It's just like committing crimes.

M: I'm sorry. I don't think I can give any advice.

J:　Oh, Mary, what do you do?

M: I'm taking advanced study for a MA.

J: Terrific! How smart you are! *Do you have nay fancy for that?*

M: *It's interesting and simple.* What I worry about is just the exam. But

sometimes the college life is dull as usual.

J: I really envy you. I hope I could do half as well as you.

M: You're flattering me! Well, I must be going.

J: Keep in touch.

Section II, Activity 1

Jenny: Are you seeing the movie "Jane Eyre", adapted from the famous

love novel?

John: No, I *don't feel like watching such kind of film*. They are not for me.

Jenny: Me neither. They are usually disappointing. But a lot of people

enjoy watching them. They think it is a good way to learn the

classics.

John: Yea, only two kinds of people *like watching such adapted movies.*

Jenny: Who are they?

John: Those who don't have to time to read books and those *who cannot*

understand the classics.

Jenny: Exactly. I *prefer reading the printed novel anyway.*

John: Me too. I think reading is much more entertaining.

Unit 2 Suggestions and Advice

Section I, Activity 2

A: Hi, Mary. You look worried. What happened?

B: Well, I'm thinking of changing my job. *Would you like to give me some advice?*

A: My boss hates me, you know. And I couldn't take working the graveyard shift anymore.

B: Oh, man, *I would suggest you talk with your boss to solve the problem.* It's hard to find a job now. And you are well paid.

A: I see. But, *hard to explain,* anyway, it can't be solved. Now, *I need you advice on the job.*

B: Mm, *what about surfing on the Net to find job vacancies*? Many people do that nowadays.

A: *Sounds good!* I will try that. Another drink?

B: No thanks. I have to go. So long.

A: So long.

Section I, Activity 3

Conversation 1:

A: I'm confused about what major I should choose.

B: What are you interested in?

A: Let me see. I'm interested in marketing and E-commerce. Oh, I also like English very much.

B: Mm, I would suggest that you major in marketing. Marketing is so important these days and all companies take marketing as one of their most important departments.

A: I agree, but I'd also like to take up a foreign language.

B: English? Sure, you can take English as your minor. You know, English will be a vital skill in your future job-hunting in globalization.

A: Good! Thank you very much. Your suggestions are very helpful for me.

Conversation 2:

A: Chew, the weekend is here at last. I really need to relax. What shall we do today?

B: I don't really know. Do you have any ideas?

A: Well, I need a new skirt. How about going shopping and hunting around with me if you have free time on your hands?

B: Oh, no! I just went shopping yesterday with Flora.

A: What a pity! What can we then?

B: Why don't we have a big dinner in the new restaurant? I heard the food in the new restaurant tastes very delicious.

A: Marvelous! I am also considering treating myself. Shall we meet at the front gate at about 6 o'clock?

B: Good! See you.

Unit 3 Doubts and Worries

Section II, Activity 1

E: Good evening, Gordon.

G: Good evening, Emma. What are you doing now?

E: I'm surfing the net.

G: Have you got anything interesting?

E: Yes. *Do you believe that* Terry Brown has achieved the Award of Excellence by the Microsoft this month?

G: Oh my goodness! You've got to be kidding. *It is incredible!* I simply can't believe what you've said.

E: *Why don't you believe what I have said?*

G: As a matter of fact, he is not an excellent student in our school. He never studies very hard.

E: In the beginning, I also rather doubted him. But *it is beyond doubt,* we must admit.

G: *I am still thinking whether it is true.* Maybe we don't know him very much.

E: Yes. We shouldn't judge a person just by his appearance.

G: Sounds reasonable. *We must believe that every person is able to make progress.*

Activity 3

W: Hi, long time no see. How have you been?

M: Oh, I've been fine, but I'm having some trouble with my son.

W: Tell me all about it.

M: Oh, he's 14 and in the past few months, he's become quieter and a bit secretive. He locks himself in his room and I think he's running around with the wrong crowd.

W: Oh, I see. What makes you think that?

M: Well, he's become friends with a couple of older boys who are in a band. And one night last weekend, he came home really late, way past his curfew.

W: Really? What happened?

M: He told me that his friend's car broke down and they had to walk home.

W: I see what you mean. I understand why you're concerned. Have you tried talking to your son about it?

M: I haven't yet. I just keep hoping it's just a phase he's going through.

W: You may be right, but it doesn't hurt to find out more about what's going on in his life.

M: You're right. I should talk to him. Sometimes, it's not easy being a parent. Thanks. It helps to get it off my chest. You're always so easy to talk to.

W: I don't know about that, but my door is always open. Stop by anytime.

Unit 4　Apologies

Section I,　Activity 2

B:　Good morning, Ms. Lee.

L:　Good morning, Brian. Why all this hurry?

B:　*I'd like to apologize to you.*

L:　*What for?* You've done a good job.

B:　Thanks for saying that. But please *Forgive me for not attending the company meeting yesterday afternoon.* I caught a bad could and had to see the doctor.

L:　*There is really no need to apologize for that.* It can happen to anyone. Well, we had to hold the meeting without you, though.

B:　I appreciate your kindness.

L:　*Forget it.* Anything I can be of help?

B:　Yes, could you tell me how you would consider my proposal about the reform of our Sales Department?

L:　Proposal? *Excuse me for not discussing that at the meeting.* I will take it into proper consideration soon.

B:　Well, that's all right. *I'm sorry to have disturbed you.*

L:　*That's OK.* See you later.

B:　See you!

Unit 5　Comparison and Contrast

Section I,　Activity 3

T : OK, Mike, I was wondering, you're from Canada, and you have lived in America, and we work together, and in our company everybody is American but you, so *how would you say Canadians are different than Americans*?

M : Well, to be honest, just to start, I'll say that *Canadians and Americans share a lot more similar qualities than they do differences*, I mean, I think Canadians have a lot more in common with Americans than they do with, even with English people who are like from Britain who were the original sort of Canadians, I suppose, a few hundred years ago, so in that way I think that like again, just to preempt it by saying we're very similar. However, *there's definitely some differences between Americans and Canadians*. First of all, I think Canadians in general are maybe a little bit more humble. Not to put this in a negative way, *they're not as willing to engage in an argument, or to argue over a point, as most of my American friends* who'll want to debate and get to the bottom of a topic. I'm feeling pretty confident about it. *Canadians would rather just sort of back off* and say, you know,

"That's, you're right. That's fine, great" but again, and I can't speak for all Canadians because it depends on your personality too, but *just to generalize, that's one difference*. Also, I would say that *Americans in general tend to be a lot more businesslike and maybe even a little more conservative*, just in the way they, I guess, view, relations, or view discussions with people, but *Canadians tend to be a little bit more liberal, a little bit more free and easy-going*, again, I'll preempt that by saying all of the Americans that I work with are quite liberal and not conservative thinking at all, but if you want to generalize, yeah, culturally, then I think *those are probably a couple of differences between the two cultures*, or people in the cultures.

T : Yeah, anything else, any other differences?

M : Well, I think, one thing that Americans tend to point to with Canadians, and *it is true to some extent*, other than our love of hockey, is sense of humor. I think Canadians in general tend to have , I wouldn't say unique, but they just tend to look at I guess, look at things with a little bit more of humor, too it, and I think the main reason for that is cause it's so bloody cold in Canada.

T : Fair enough. Thanks Mike.

Section III,   Activity 1

T: So, Mark, I heard that you are going to be leaving Tokyo pretty soon.

M: I am. I'm getting out of the city.

T: Ah, man, so when you go back to America, are you going to live in a big city like Atlanta or Birmingham?

M: Well, I am from Birmingham, which is a kind of medium sized city, but there's a lot of access to the countryside, cause Birmingham is a medium sized city but Alabama is very rural, so lots of mountains, lots of countryside and I'm actually looking forward to getting into that setting again.

T: Oh, man. I don't know dude. I grew up on a farm, and I lived way out in the country growing up, and I can't stand the country now.

M: Really?

T: Yeah. I've lived in big cities: San Francisco, London, Bangkok, Tokyo.

M: But don't you miss like the, you know, fresh air, and the views. Don't you just tired of concrete jungles, and buildings .

T: Ah, that's true. I mean, when you're in the country, you have fresh air and you do have, you know, the beauty, and this and that, but it's just boring. It's the same five people.

M: It is true, but actually I find it's harder to meet people in a big city, because there is so many people, so you're, nobody really cares to stop and talk to you because there is a million other people around, but if you're in a town, a small town, or out in the country, the few people you do meet, you form a good relationship with.

T: Yeah, that's somewhat true, but there's just no energy. You know the countries slow. You can't just go to any restaurant at any time,you can't, you know, go see a museum, or go see a ball game or go to a nightclub and it's a just a lot of sitting around.

M: Well, that's true and, if I do, every time I go back to the country, I always miss those things, like a museum, and you know, concerts and things like that, but I'm just able to relax so much more when I'm out in a rural setting.

T: Well, I hope you have a good time.

M: Thanks.

Unit 6 Agreement and Disagreement

Section I,   Activity 2

D: Well, no one can resist the temptation of soccer, it's really fantastic.

J: Mm, could be. *But you carry it too far, don't you?*

D: Football has been a part of modern civilization. I'd like to say that soccer is the most exciting sport.

J: *I see what you mean*, but a lot of games are very exciting. I love basketball. Michael Jordan, what a great name! Although he has retired, the Chicago Bulls as well as the NBA will live with me forever.

D: So you're a diehard basketball fan?

J: *Absolutely.* You are a good football player?

D: No, but I like playing football. I play every day and always watch matched on television.

J: I hate watching football games, it's slow and so few goals are scored in ninety minutes.

D: *You're kidding.* Your weird opinion surprised me very much. Football is the most popular sport in the world. Every football player might become a world-renown star.

J: *I'm not sure I can agree.* Tennis isn't less popular than football.

D: Maybe, but you know The World Cup is for football.

J: OK, *let's agree to disagree.*

Unit 7 Invitation

Section I, Activity 3

L: Hi, Beth. I've been thinking of asking you *if you have nay plans for the Chinese National Day.*

B: No, not really.

L: Well, *I was planning to have a party at my house.*

B: Sure, *I' like to come.* Who are you inviting?

L: Some young teachers from the department and three of your American students. That way you can practice your Chinese, too.

B: That's a great idea. What can I bring?

L: Let's see. I'll practice everything Chinese, and …

B: Why don't I make a potato salad?

L: *That's terrific!*

B: Is there any way I can help?

L: Well, I should let them know about the party, so they won't plan anything else.

B: Right. I'll be seeing Bob and Jane tomorrow. Do you want me to tell them about it?

L: Oh, please.

B: *What time do you want them to show up?*

L: About five. I'd like everyone to come early so that you can talk before dinner. Oh, and one more thing, could you ask Bob to bring his records?

B: *Sure thing.*

L: Thanks. Bye-bye.

B: Bye.

Unit 8 Describing a person / an event or an experience

Section I,   Activity 2

W: Oh, are those pictures of your kids?

M: Yes. These are my three daughters and these are my two sons.

W: Your sons look so alike. Are they similar in personality, too?

M: It's funny you ask that. My wife and I are always saying how different they are from one another, even though they're the closest in age. Sergey, the younger one, is moody and a little timid, while his older brother, Dennis, is talkative and cheerful all the time.

W: That's really interesting. You know, I have an older sister and we're only a year apart, but we have very different personalities, too. When I was little, I was bad-tempered and I always fought with my brothers and sisters, while my sister was a little angel. She was always patient and generous. I really looked up to her.

M: It's hard for me to believe that you were ever bad-tempered. You're so even-keeled now. Me, on the other hand, I was a selfish and stubborn kid. I'm surprised that my parents put up with me.

W: I'm sure you're exaggerating. All kids are a little selfish and stubborn, think. Good thing most of us grow out of it as we get older.

M: Well, that may be true, but according to my wife and kids, I'm still the most stubborn person in the world. They may be right.

Section II,   Activity 1

M: Hi, Joe, this is Maggie, Maggie Graham.

J: Oh, hi, Maggie. How are you?

M: I'm fine. How are you?

J: Fine.

M: Listen, um…*I want to ask you some questions about Alex Wilson —* You know him, don't you?

J: Sure.

M: *What's he like?*

J: Well, why are you asking about Alex?

M: Well, I want to try and get a part time job at his store …

J: Oh, well, Alex's nice guy …

M: Mm-hmm.

J: I mean *he'll give you decent hours, a decent pay, and plenty of breaks.*

M: Well, that sounds good. Um, *what does he look like?* I've got to meet him at the Sunset restaurant for lunch and I can't remember.

J: Oh, well he's about mid-thirty.

M: Uh-huh.

J: … six-foot-two…

M: Right.

J: … Oh, *he's well-built, mature and speaks with magnetic voice.*

M: Oh, sounds kind of handsome.

J: Mm.

M: Um, is he a formal kind of guy, or does he dress casually?

J: Oh, he rarely dresses casually. *He always wears three-piece suits and ties* — dresses very much in style.

M: Oh, I see, I better dress up then … OK, thanks a lot. Bye!

J: Bye! Have a good time!

Unit 9 Problems and Solutions

Section I, Activity 2

It's easy to spread germs that cause colds, flu and other illnesses. According to the US centers for disease control and prevention, this is why you need to protect yourself and *take steps to avoid infecting others.* The agency recently published a list of recommendations to stay healthy. It advises to *avoid close contact* with people who are sick. If you are sick, stay home. When you cough or sneeze, *cover your mouth and nose* with a tissue. Frequently wash your hands. Avoid *touching your eyes, nose or mouth.* Clean and disinfect often-used surfaces at home, work or school. Get plenty of sleep and r*egular physical activity.* Drink plenty of nonalcoholic fluids to stay well-hydrated. Finally, maintain *a healthy, well-balanced diet.*

Activity 3

L: This is it. I'm quitting smoking for good.

M: Good for you. Are you going cold turkey?

L: No, *I tried that, but it didn't work.* I craved cigarettes too much.

M: *How about nicotine gum?* Have you tried that?

L: Yes, but I didn't like the side effects. It irritated my throat.

M: That's too bad. *I suppose you've tried nicotine patches, too?*

L: Yes, I have. I became addicted to the patches and couldn't wean myself off of them. *I just traded one addiction for another.*

M: And electronic cigarettes?

L: They only made me want to smoke a real cigarette. *They were no help at all.*

M: So, what now?

L: I'm going to try hypnosis. I hear that it works for some people.

M: And *if that doesn't work?*

L: The last resort is acupuncture. Some people say that's effective for quitting smoking.

M: *If you say so.* Sometimes the cure is truly worse than the disease!

Unit 10 Comment on News

Section II, Activity 1

M: *This is just so crazy!*

J: What?

M: This story I'm reading.

K: So tell us.

M: A man within a wheelchair crossing the road in front of a lorry at some traffic lights. Somehow, the back of the wheelchair got stuck on the front of the lorry. When the lorry started moving, it took the wheelchair and the man with it!

K: *You're joking!*

M: The driver drove for several miles at 80 kilometers an hour before he stopped at a garage. The man was unhurt because his seat belt had stopped him falling out.

J: *What a terrible story!* Thank goodness the man was all right.

M: The police asked the driver if he'd realized he has a passenger. The driver said he had no idea at all.

M: Do you want to hear another one? A funny one this time.

K: Go on.

M: A woman reported that her car had been stolen and she'd left her mobile phone in the car. The policeman suggested calling the mobile. When he did, the thief answered it. The policeman told the thief that he was answering an ad in the paper and that he wanted to buy the car. And the thief agreed to sell it.

J: *He didn't!*

M: So they arranged to meet and the thief was arrested and the woman got her car back.

J: *A happy ending!*

M: *You get these great stories in the paper* — I always read them.

References

[1] 辛斌 . 研究生英语高级口语 [M]. 上海：复旦大学出版社，2009 年 .

[2] 李雪，李铁红，范宏博 . 社交英语口语大全 [M]. 北京机械工业出版社，2014 年 .

[3] 李华东 . 新世纪英语口语教程 [M]. 北京：外语教学与研究出版社，2013 年 .

[4] 王秋雨 . 英语听说教程（第二册）[M]. 北京：北京大学出版社，2009 年 .

[5] 剑桥英语教师宝典：课堂讨论 [M]. 天津：南开大学出版社，2007 年 .

[6] 剑桥英语教师宝典 – 通过演戏说英语 [M]. 天津：南开大学出版社，2007 年 .

[7] Penny Ur, Discussion that Work: Task-centered fluency practice, Cambridge University Press, 1981.

[8] Simon Greenall, 文秋芳 . New Standard College English Real Communication: Listening and Speaking 2, Foreign Language Teaching and Research Press & Macmillan Publishers Ltd, 2009 年 .

[9] http://tefltastic.wordpress.com

[10] https://www.teach-this.com / functional-activities-worksheets / describing-character-personality